PUBLISHED ON THE FOUNDATION
ESTABLISHED IN MEMORY OF
PHILIP HAMILTON McMILLAN
OF THE CLASS OF 1894
YALE COLLEGE

UGARITIC MYTHOLOGY

A Study of Its Leading Motifs

JULIAN OBERMANN
Professor of Semitic Languages
in Yale University

NEW HAVEN
YALE UNIVERSITY PRESS
LONDON · GEOFFREY CUMBERLEGE · OXFORD UNIVERSITY PRESS
1948

Printed in the United States of America

THE PHILIP HAMILTON McMILLAN MEMORIAL PUBLICATION FUND

The present volume is the thirty-seventh work published by the Yale University Press on the Philip Hamilton McMillan Memorial Publication Fund. This Foundation was established December 12, 1922, by a gift to Yale University in pursuance of a pledge announced on Alumni University Day in February, 1922, of a Fund of $100,000 bequeathed to James Thayer McMillan and Alexis Caswell Angell, as Trustees, by Mrs. Elizabeth Anderson McMillan, of Detroit, to be devoted by them to the establishment of a memorial in honor of her husband.

He was born in Detroit, Michigan, December 28, 1872, prepared for college at Phillips Academy, Andover, and was graduated from Yale in the Class of 1894. As an undergraduate he was a leader in many of the college activities of his day, and within a brief period of his graduation was called upon to assume heavy responsibilities in the management and direction of numerous business enterprises in Detroit, where he was also a Trustee of the Young Men's Christian Association and of Grace Hospital. His untimely death, from heart disease, on October 4, 1919, deprived his city of one of its leading citizens and his University of one of its most loyal sons.

To

CHARLES CUTLER TORREY

In Faith and Devotion

ACKNOWLEDGMENT

It is the author's pleasant duty to express indebtedness to M. Claude F. A. Schaeffer, director of the excavations at Ras Shamra, for his courtesy in approving the reproduction of the plates used in this volume.

PREFACE

UP to less than twenty years ago, virtually nothing was known about the ancient kingdom that had borne the name " Ugarit " and had flourished in northern Syria some fifteen centuries before the beginning of our era. Nothing whatsoever was known about its language, its people, its civilization, or even its exact location. Indeed, except for a few passing references to it found in documents of the second pre-Christian millennium—Egyptian, Amarnaian, Hittite—we should have remained unaware of its one-time existence altogether. During the past two decades, however, the bliss of our ignorance of the long-lost kingdom has been severely shaken.

Early in 1930 the scholarly world was served notice of startling discoveries made by a French archaeological expedition at Ras Shamra—a sloping Arab village or hamlet in the vicinity of the Mediterranean seaport of Latakia, in northern Syria. A mere accident had precipitated the undertaking: in the spring of 1928 a peasant happened to strike with his plough some stone slabs that proved to roof an ancient tomb. Fortunately, the chance discovery was brought to the attention of the French authorities in Beirut; and as early as the following spring, an expedition was sufficiently organized, under the auspices of the Académie des Inscriptions et Belles-Lettres, to begin excavating the mound of Ras Shamra and to continue its work each year thereafter.

But it was only during the third campaign, in 1931, that evidence came to light which led to the identification of that mound as the site of the capital of ancient Ugarit. And when, in 1939, the work of the excavators was stopped because of the war, the accumulated wealth of their archaeological and inscriptional finds had become of vital concern to nearly every department of the science of antiquity. They had presented the world of scholars with materials and enigmas destined to engage their ingenuity for many years to come. In less than a decade, then, the study of the ancient Near East found itself expanded and revitalized by an entirely new field of philological research—the field of Ugaritic.

The successive publication of gradually exhumed epigraphic materials has been met, from the initial publication on, speedily—sometimes indeed too speedily—with active response and critical reaction by an ever wider circle of students, in articles, monographs, and books dedicated to one or another aspect of the Ugaritic finds. Savants of many lands, including a sizable number of American scholars, cooperated with their French colleagues in the enormous task imposed upon them by the new field of research—the task of deciphering a new system of writing, of analyzing the structure of a new language, of translating and interpreting a new literature, of comprehending and appraising a new culture.*

An auspicious beginning toward discharging this challenging task was made by the rapid and brilliant solution of the riddle of the new script. It was found to be executed in the manner of cuneiform writing, that is, impressed by a stylus upon soft clay, yet to consist of

* A convenient survey of all the Ugaritic materials, as well as of the far-flung scholarly literature, published up to 1944 (?) may be found in "Index bibliographique" of R. de Langhe, *Les Textes de Ras Shamra-Ugarit et leurs rapports avec le milieu biblique de l'Ancien Testament* (Universitas Catholica Lovaniensis, Gembloux-Paris, 1944-45), I, xvi-lvii.

but few signs as compared with Mesopotamian cuneiform or Egyptian hieroglyphics. The decipherers started from two assumptions: (*a*) that, in view of their close proximity, in time and space, to the "land of Canaan," the people of Ugarit must have been Semites and, accordingly, their script must have been used to record a Semitic dialect; and (*b*) that, in consideration of the small number of signs it employed, it obviously represented a system of writing based on the alphabetic principle. Since both assumptions happened to be correct, the task of deciphering was successfully completed, for all practical purposes, as early as the summer of 1930, on the basis of the very first publication of Ugaritic clay tablets. There remained, however—and, in fact, there still remains—the problem of the position of the new script within the evolution of alphabetic writing and, what is especially vexing, of the relationship between the cuneiform alphabet of the Semites of Ugarit and the linear alphabet of the Semites of near-by but younger Phoenicia, from which the great majority of known alphabets, including our own, ultimately derive.

Much less rapid and less assured has been the progress made toward clearing the riddle of the new dialect. Here, too, the early realization that Ugaritic was not in reality a new language, plain and simple, but merely a new specimen of Semitic speech, proved to be a stroke of very good fortune. For, with nothing else to go by except that realization or assumption, certain common features of phonemics, morphology, and syntax, as well as a number of basic vocables, could soon be discerned in the new dialect by the naked eye, as it were. Less common elements could gradually be comprehended on the basis of more or less unmistakable counterparts found in certain Semitic areas or even confined to a single area, that is, on the basis of counterparts peculiarly Akkadian, or characteristically Arabic, or typically Hebrew. Almost ad libitum, scholars could select words, phrases, or even whole sentences, by which they might demonstrate that Ugaritic is almost " just like Hebraic " or from which they might deduce grammatical norms of the new dialect.

Although great strides have thus been made, and are continuing to be made, at best the mere foundation has been laid bare to date. The structure itself, in all its depth and breadth, is yet to be cleared. To some extent, but by no means entirely, this has been conditioned by the fact that—apart only from syllables involving the glottal stop—Ugaritic writing does not provide for graphic representation of vowels, so that such vital questions as concern word formation, inflectional endings, or weak verbs, always depend on conjecture. Together with an abundance of enclitic and proclitic particles, this absence of vowel signs has made it frequently impossible to determine as much as the bare identity, the essential components, of a given vocable. Very often, again, a word consisting of one or two consonants may be identified with one of several different vocables—sometimes with as many as half a dozen—each of which can be shown to be used elsewhere in Semitic. Moreover, there has seemed to be strong indication of peculiarities, syntactic as well as semantic, which Ugaritic either had developed independently or had shared with Semitic dialects that have come down to us in greatly limited scope, such as Old Phoenecian and Old Aramaic, or have not reached us at all, such as Amorite.

As could not be otherwise, the slow and equivocal penetration into the grammatical and lexical structure of the new dialect has rendered the task of translating and interpreting the new literature proportionately slow and equivocal. In addition, the pursuit of this task has been seriously hampered by two circumstances: (*a*) an external circumstance—the lacunar and fragmentary condition in which nearly all of the more important, larger tablets have been found; and (*b*) an internal circumstance—the all but complete uncertainty surrounding such intangibles as hints, allusions, implications, whether cultic, cultural, technical, historical, social, or ethnic. As a result, the student of Ugaritic texts, particularly those of epical narrative, has found himself ever faced with a duel set of difficulties, (*a*) those of the idiom proper and (*b*) those of the context, in the immediate as well as the larger sense of the word. Small wonder that the first attempts, and not only the first, to translate Ugaritic documents have been in the nature of indecisive groping, and that for a long time virtually no passage of any length has appeared plausible or coherent from beginning to end and in every detail, so that scholars have had to resort to offering translations in which more or less numerous elements were adorned with question marks or left untranslated altogether.

Not only have the criterion of context, on the one hand, and the linguistic control of the text, on the other, both proved to be equally difficult and equally essential prerequisites to the task of translation and interpretation, but they have been found to depend on one another as their sole test of validity or invalidity. Words, phrases, or sentences that could easily be analyzed when considered by themselves, and hence could be used to demonstrate points of grammatical theory, have often proved obscure and unwieldy when submitted to the contextual test of a given literary unit in which they were found. Consequently, when, by the help of a postulated interpretation, the context of a literary unit seemed tolerably clear, it has often led to a revised analysis of grammatical and semantic elements that had been deduced *suis locis*, that is, without regard to the question of context. It is fair to say that such assured progress as has been made—and this is by no means inconsiderable—has been achieved by repeated reciprocal testing of the kind just indicated; that is, by the linguistic analysis and the criterion of context continually brought to bear one upon the other. Of course, the immediate context of a given scene, episode, or dialogue is only a first step—comparable to grammatical or semantic deductions based on isolated passages, without reference to the textual material in its entirety. For the purpose of a truly valid translation and interpretation of the new documents, an ever wider extension of the criterion of context has proved to be a *sine qua non*—extension beyond the given literary unit to the whole narrative of which it is a part, beyond the narrative to the cycle to which it belongs, and indeed further to the entire cultural realm of Ugaritic literature taken as a whole.

It is only natural that, once Ugaritic was established as an offspring of Semitic stock, attempts should have been made to define it more closely by inquiring as to which branch of the family it represented. Merely by its geographic position, as well as by less palpable factors to be mentioned presently, scholars have generally been inclined to identify the new dialect as Canaanite, so much so that in recent publications almost anything Ugaritic—the language, literature, folklore, cult, mythology, prosody—may be found referred to simply as "Old Canaanite," in contrast, that is, to younger Canaanite dialects and cultures, such as Phoenician, Hebrew, Moabite. Other scholars, guided by different considerations, have been led to see in Ugaritic close dialectic kinship to East Canaanite, or Amorite, while still others have pointed to its affinities with Aramaic. None of the advanced theories, however, has appeared sufficiently conclusive to find universal acceptance; and, from what has been said above, all attempts of this kind would seem decidedly premature. Although an important and urgent problem in itself, the particular dialectic identity of Ugaritic is bound to remain a moot question until, and unless, a more solid understanding of its structure has been obtained than is possible at present—an understanding of its moods and tenses, of its word formation, of it particles, of its sentence construction, especially with regard to coordination and subordination.

To the extent of our limited knowledge, it is true, Ugaritic does appear to re-echo in Hebrew with extraordinary persistence, incalculably more so, at any rate, than in any other known sphere of Semitic speech. So clearly is this the case that for a time it has seriously threatened to deter and encumber the advance of Ugaritic studies, the early reaction of many scholars having been that we deal here with something very much " like Hebraic." But the sheer fact remains that for a critical approach to the syntax, style, and prosody of the new dialect, to say nothing of vocabulary and locutions, classical Hebrew has proved an invaluable guide; while, conversely, a great deal has already been gained from Ugaritic—and, by every indication, a great deal more is yet to be gained—for a new critical study of the Old Testament. This, however, need not necessarily indicate genetic affinity between Ugaritic and Hebrew beyond the mere fact that both are Semetic dialects. One need

2

think only of the truly remarkable re-echoing of Arabic in medieval Syriac, Hebrew, and Ethiopic, under the impact of Islam. All that can be said with impunity is that, either directly or indirectly (say, through the mediation of Phoenicia), a very close and lasting bond must be assumed to have existed between the sphere of the new dialect and that of Hebrew to account for the extraordinarily vivid and manifold contact between the two idioms; specifically, a bond between the Semites of Ugarit and the pre-Israelite, or Canaanite, Semites of Palestine. If so, the Israelite conquerors of the " land of Canaan " would have adopted not only the vernacular Hebrew of the conquered, but their poetic style, their literary vocabulary and locutions, their prosody, and even some of their standard narrative and hymn patterns, as well.

Even with but a sketchy appreciation of the Ugaritic texts it is possible to see that, above all else, it is the new species of literature that makes the finds of Ras Shamra rank among the foremost discoveries in modern times. Indeed the barest kind of survey of the material so far brought to light suffices to make one realize, in particular, that the new literature signifies nothing less than an entirely new turn, in fact a new epoch, in the religious evolution of the ancient Near East.

Seen externally, the exhumed epigraphic material divides itself into two groups of tablets: a group of smaller tablets, usually inscribed in a single column of, sometimes, as few as ten or twelve lines of writing; and a group of much larger tablets, inscribed in four, six, or eight columns, with often as many as sixty or more lines to a column. A goodly number of the smaller tablets could be seen to be ritual in content, while others appear to be of administrative or civic character. By contrast, the larger tablets have proved to represent epical narratives or rather sections of such narratives, a given poem being often too long to be inscribed on a single tablet. Only one or two of the narratives seem to concern human beings as well as deities, while all other narratives deal exclusively with the doings of gods—the mythology of the gods of Ugarit. Again, in the ritual tablets frequent reference is made to deities named El and Baal. From the epical narratives, on the other hand, we learn that although El held the foremost position in the pantheon, the great hero of the epic, around whom nearly all dramatic action evolves, was Baal. Second only in importance to these two gods, we soon come to see, were two goddesses named Athirat, that is, the biblical Asherah, and Anat.

Thus the Ras Shamra excavations have yielded the first authentic specimens of pagan Semitic literature that have ever reached us either from Canaan itself or from its immediate vicinity. Nor is it admissible to assume that the specimens now before us exemplify the true scope of the literary achievements of the Semites of Ugarit. It would be very odd indeed if the people that had reached so high a standard in the field of epical narrative should have failed completely to develop similar ambitions and capabilities in related fields—in recording their past history, in committing to writing their cosmology, in codifying their laws, their prayers, their incantations. Further excavations, probing new sites of the area, may very well present us with specimens of Ugaritic literature essentially supplementing those discovered hitherto. And if only for this reason, resumption of the excavations at Ras Shamra should be recognized as one of the most vital archaeological desiderata of the day.

But even when judged by the evidence on hand, the literature of Ugarit may be seen to have developed to a high degree of versatility; yet, by the same evidence, this far-flung pagan literature appears to have evolved entirely in the sphere of religion—either in the realm of the gods, pure and simple, or in that of the dependency relationship between the frailty of man and the power of the gods. It is indeed as if the boldest dream of a learned theologian had come true. For students of antiquity have long since postulated a situation of the kind evidenced in the Ugaritic tablets, while the divine names just mentioned have been familiar even to lay readers of the Scriptures. Yet, prior to the discovery of the new literature, all information bearing on the pagan religion of the Semites of Canaan had been vague and tenuous in itself and derived from secondary or even tertiary sources. Thus testimony to a highly developed mythology of the ancient Phoenicians could indeed be gleaned from the traditions compiled by Sanchunyaton, who is said to have lived before the Trojan War and to have obtained his data from temple archives and inscriptions composed in archaic Phoenician script and language. But these data—on which much light has now been shed by the Ugaritic finds—were preserved only through the medium of a Greek rendering of Philo of Byblos, which in turn reached us only in the sadly abridged and dubious excerpts incorporated in the *Praeparatio evangelica* of Eusebius.

The data on the pagan religion of Canaan as contained in the biblical writings are much more weighty in accumulative volume than those of Sanchunyaton, but, at the same time, they are much less specific, less concrete, and rendered all but useless to the objective historian by the element of incessant reproof and irreconcilable polemics. The one outstanding fact of overwhelming importance and unanswerable certainty is that protagonists of a pure worship of the God of Sinai held it to be forever contaminated, undermined, and endangered in its very existence by the worship of the gods of Canaan. A nonliterary prophet of the ninth century challenges the people to make a clear-cut decision and to choose once and for all between Yahweh and Baal. The work of the great literary prophets of the eighth century might be characterized as a series of stirring variations on the theme of that challenge. A Judean king, of the seventh century, immortalized his name by banishing from the temple of Jerusalem "all the vessels that were made for Baal and Asherah." In the fifth century, members of the Jewish colony of Elephantine are found to swear by Anat-Yahu—a syncretism that would be inconceivable unless the colonists had brought it with them from their Judean homeland.

But what exactly was the religion of Baal? What was the meaning of the coupling of Baal and Asherah, of Anat and Yahu? What was it that had rendered the pagan cult of Canaan so irresistible to the rank and file of the people of Yahweh for so many generations? And by what compromise and adjustment did Yahwism emerge victorious in the end notwithstanding the attraction of Baalism—an attraction so great as to have made seers and prophets all but despair of the lot of their nation?

Biblical scholars have long been faced with these questions, and have tried to answer them by such conjectures as they deemed warranted despite insufficient bases of objective and first-hand factual material. It is only now, in the light of the new literature of Ugarit, that we may look forward to gaining a clear insight into the intricate problem. For here we have come upon the mythology of Baalism in epic detail. Here, in the rediscovered pagan lore of Semites from the vicinity of Canaan, we learn from their own testimony, preserved in contemporary records, about their beliefs and notions concerning Baal, Athirat-Asherah, Anat, and many other deities. Here, in the epos of Baal, we learn what his worshippers, in solemn metrical chants, had told about his life and death and resurrection, about his alliances and enmities, about his fears and ambitions. And we have seen already how incalculably close a bond must be recognized as having existed between the mythology of Ugarit and that of pre-Israelite Palestine. We have seen this from the persistent literary re-echoing of Ugaritic even in the writings of the Hebrew Scriptures; that is, from its re-echoing in the writings of avowed deadly antagonists of Baalism many centuries after Ugarit itself had vanished from the face of the earth.

The following study involves but a small section of Ugaritic mythology. It has grown out of an attempt to analyze the mythological narrative of the so-called Anat Poem (*5AB*). Inscribed on a tablet of six columns and well preserved on the whole—except for a number of lacunae and defacements—the narrative has long seemed enigmatic with regard to its main purport, and therefore also with regard to the meaning and implication of its individual scenes and episodes. Only toward the end of the tablet, one or two scenes could readily be seen to concern the building saga, but no connection seemed apparent either between those scenes and the rest of the poem or between the other episodes of the narrative taken by themselves. Failing to uncover its general trend and topic, and thus lacking the criterion afforded by an over-all context, any analysis of the narrative would have been doomed beforehand to remain a haphazard experiment, certainly as to the appraisal of its literary composition, inevitably also as to the understanding of its grammatical and lexical details.

It was only upon recognition of the main intent and purpose of the poet that an attempt to analyze the poem did become feasible; namely, upon the recognition that throughout the text of the tablet, and not merely in this or that of its components, we are faced with a narrative dedicated to the building saga, or rather with the beginning of such a narrative. In consequence, the designation of the composition as an " Anat Poem " had to be abandoned as meaningless and indeed misleading. It served well enough as a makeshift so long as the true character of the poem remained elusive; it was justifiable only on the ground that the goddess Anat does appear to play an important part in the proceedings, but on no other ground whatever. As a further consequence, it became necessary to bring to bear on the analysis other Ugaritic poems related to the building saga, especially the poem of a tablet (*2AB*) which, to a considerable extent, could be seen to cover the same ground as that of the narrative before us. After the analysis had been virtually completed, a new Ugaritic fragment became available (*3AB C*) that proved to contain a significant and hitherto unknown episode bearing on the building saga and to lend support to some of the conclusions that had been reached in the course of the inquiry.

Decisive as the criterion furnished by the over-all context has been, its greatest usefulness has appeared to be of a negative nature. In the main, it has helped to eliminate previous considerations, whether exegetical or grammatical, that would have rendered a given scene or episode pointedly out of keeping with the general purport of the narrative. By way of a more positive test, only such text units have been adduced, to serve as direct or indirect witnesses to the analysis, as could be translated from beginning to end and in every particular. If the translations thus offered should be found acceptable, this alone might justify publication of the present study.

The question of motifs has proved a constant stumbling block even in this preliminary inquiry into the new mythology. What had started as a study of a single narrative of the Ugaritic building saga—and this, as will be seen, only the beginning of such a narrative—developed all but inadvertently into a study of the saga's basic motifs. I soon came to realize that to ignore this question would have meant depriving the analysis of its ultimate test. I am satisfied, however, that the motifs as crystallized in the present inquiry will be found to underlie the building saga as a whole in all its known versions. Indeed, it is very safe to expect that the same motifs will prove acute and productive in Ugaritic mythology in general, although additional motifs may of course emerge in the process of a more comprehensive study.

J. O.

CONTENTS

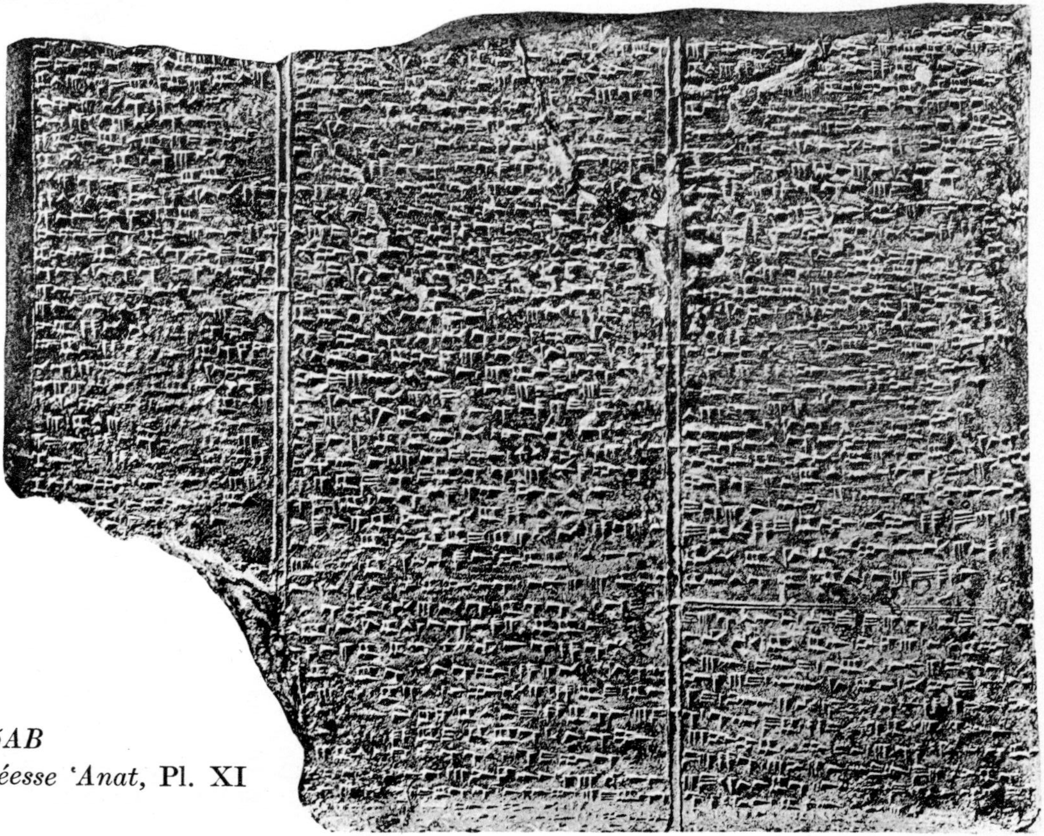

Obverse of *5AB*
From Ch. Virolleaud, *La Déesse ʿAnat*, Pl. XI

UGARITIC MYTHOLOGY

I. INTRODUCTORY CONSIDERATIONS

On the Building Saga in General

THE story of how Baal planned to build a splendid house for himself, how he plotted to obtain consent to his plan from his father, the supreme god El, and how in the end he achieved his objective, appears to have formed a central theme—perhaps we should say *the* central theme—of the mythological folklore current among the Semites of Ugarit. In addition to El and Baal, the epical material involves a considerable number of other deities, both major and minor: Athirat, Anat, Mot, Shapash, Hayin, Gepen-and-Ugar, Qaddish-and-Amrar, Baal's three "brides," Athtar, Prince Sea, and still others.

Only a few of these gods represent *dramatis personae* of the epic on a par with Baal and El. Much in the foreground of the stage, and playing decisive parts in the dramatic action, are three deities, all of whom are allied with Baal in his scheme, variously contributing to its promotion: his mother, the gentle Lady Athirat; his sister, the ferocious and ruthless Anat; the master-builder Hayin, who, when the plot has sufficiently advanced, is summoned to come, and does come, all the way from Egypt to help bring Baal's ambition to final realization.

An equally prominent part is played by Mot, Baal's arch enemy. But, as far as the building legend is concerned, it is an essentially negative part, involving no direct action and played, as it were, off stage. Only at the end of the process does Mot enter the picture, but even now his part is a passive one. After his plan has come to a successful conclusion, Baal sends word to Mot to say

> My house I have built [of silver,
> Of gold I have wrought my pa]lace! [1]

It is, then, as if part of Baal's scheme was to keep it a secret from Mot until it became an accomplished fact. Indeed, it is all but impossible to escape the inference that the latent enmity between Baal and Mot came to a head—exploding into the gruesome struggle of which the Ugaritic saga has preserved for us so graphic a description [2]—as a result of Baal's success in his building scheme; and that, conversely, in having achieved this success, Baal had won an asset which was to enhance his ultimate victory in that struggle.

Nor is Mot the only adversary of Baal, who, had it been in his power, would surely have endeavored to frustrate the plan. Throughout the narratives, we shall see, emphatic reference is made to enemies and rivals of Baal, who, it is implied, would be inimical or dangerous

[1] *2AB* 8:40-42; the badly damaged passage has been restored on the basis of *2AB* 6:36-38.

The several cycles of Ugaritic tablets—*Aliyan Baal* (*AB*), *Daniel* (*D*), and *Keret* (*K*)—are quoted from the text editions published by Charles Virolleaud; for details, see the List of Abbreviations. For *Keret*, see also H. L. Ginsberg, *LK*, in *BASOR*, Supplementary Studies, Nos. 2-3. Of studies bearing on *5AB*, the following may be noted here: R. Dussaud, in *RHR*, 1937, pp. 121 ff.; 1938, pp. 133 ff.; W. F. Albright, in *BASOR*, *70* (1938), 18 ff.; J. Aistleitner, in *ZAW*, 1939, pp. 193 ff.; A. Goetze, in *BASOR*, *93* (1944), 17 ff.; A. Herdner, in *RÉS-Babyloniaca*, 1942-45, pp. 33 ff.; C. H. Gordon, *PL*, in *Orientalia*, *12* (1943), 31 ff.; also *UG*. Reference is also made to the writer's "Incubation," in *JAOS*, *65* (1946), Supplement No. 6, and "Negation," in *JBL*, *65* (1946), 233 ff.

[2] *1AB* 6:16 ff.; cf. *PL*, p. 40.

to his undertaking and on whose destruction or submission the success of Baal's plan depends. From the fragment of a tablet designated as *3AB* we learn how Hayin helped Baal destroy an enemy named " Prince Sea " and " Chieftan River " by providing him with a " staff " or " rod," presumably wrought of metal. The physical destruction, it is explicitly indicated, is a prerequisite by which Baal would obtain " kingdom eternal," " reign for ever and ever." [3] In short, the deities who have allied themselves with Baal have, *ipso facto*, entered a conspiracy against other gods: in promoting his plan to erect a house for himself, they connive against Baal's enemies, the most outstanding and most dangerous of whom is Mot.

Baal's scheme appears to have involved also a measure of conspiracy and connivance against El himself. The epic tells how Anat, upon receiving Baal's commission to take his request to El, made a statement to the effect that, should the supreme god prove unsympathetic, she would break down his resistance by submitting him to dire physcal punishment " unless he grant a house to Baal like the gods." [4] Nor did the conniving stop here. Baal's appeal to El does not contain, in any of its several occurrences, a single word to indicate what kind of house he intended to build once he had secured his father's permission in principle.[5] Apparently, then, the point was to keep El ignorant of what was to be the intrinsic feature of the house, and thus to obtain his consent under false pretenses. In fact,

[3] See below, n. 23 and n. 81. [4] " Negation," pp. 240 f.

[5] With but minor variants (see below, n. 31 and n. 32), the appeal occurs twice in *5AB* (E : 1-6; 43-51) and twice in *2AB* (1 : 4-19; 4-5: 47-57); relatively best preserved is the last mentioned occurrence; cf. below, n. 7.

El gives unmistakable expression to his ignorance when, in yielding to Athirat's plea in Baal's behalf, he says:

> Lo, let a handmaiden of Athirat ready bricks,
> (Thus) a house may be built for Baal like the gods.[6]

Yet, when on the strength of this utterance Baal and his allies feel free to proceed with the actual building, they provide, not for a handmaiden to ready some bricks, but for the master-builder Hayin to smelt " silver by the thousands " and " gold by the myriads."

So much then seems clear—an alliance-enmity motif appears to dominate the building saga and indeed Ugaritic mythology as a whole: the motif of a trust and concord between Baal and certain gods, and the corollary motif of inherent opposition between him and certain other gods. While both corollaries of the motif are equally apparent throughout the mythological poems, it is in the nature of things that the enmity is the more outspoken and dynamic, no doubt also the more primary, factor in the epical development. Obviously, this enmity is irreconcilable; it cannot be resolved by mutual agreement and compromise; it can be terminated only by annihilation or unqualified submission of the enemy. Whether we deal here with an etiological reflection of social-ethnic conditions, such as long-standing feuds and rivalries between different Ugaritic clans, or of the antinomous forces in nature—life and death, fertility and aridness—is a question that need not interest us here. The important thing is that alliance and enmity between gods is the decisive motif in the building epic, although other, perhaps secondary, motifs will have to be discerned ere we may fully comprehend all the implications of the dramatic saga.

[6] *2AB* 4-5 : 61-63; *PL*, p. 44.

The truth is that a great many questions still need clarification, not only in respect to a number of details but to some of the more salient features as well. This is due partly to the lamentable condition in which the pertinent texts have been preserved, partly to the fact that, while the study of Ugaritic has come a long way since the first discoveries at Ras Shamra, our knowledge is still inadequate in respect to its vocabulary, its syntax and, above all, its technical-cultural implications. Very often one finds oneself facing a situation not unlike that which would confront a reader of Christian literature unfamiliar with the plain meaning of such expressions as "the Son of Man," "the Eucharist," "the Sabbath," "the Paschal Lamb," "the Kingdom of Heaven," and the like. As a result, we are often unable to grasp even the rudimentary ideas implied in the epic as a whole or in its incidental turns and episodes.

Thus for example, we do not comprehend the full meaning of the "complaint"

> Woe, there is no house unto Baal like (unto) the gods

—a complaint that seems to signify something like the leitmotif of the epic.[7] We simply do not know whether the implication is that it just happened that Baal had not yet acquired a house; or that he was not allowed to have a house or the kind of house he wanted; or perhaps that he had lost, or had been driven out of, his house.

[7] The rendering of *any* as "complaint" or "lament" (first suggested, I believe, by Ginsberg) is now borne out by *2K* 1-2 : 6 f. (also 106 f.): *tbkyk ab ġr b'l . . . any ḥl-m adr*, "there will weep for thee, father, the mount of Baal . . . there will lament the exalted area"; cf. *LK*, p. 26, and the note a. l. (p. 44). I have always taken *wn* (< *wēn* < *wain*) as an equivalent of Aramaic *wai*, Arabic *wail*; a "complaint" or "lament" (*any*) is "exclaimed" (*yṣḥ*) by means of "woe, alas" (*wn*). For the full wording of Baal's plea to El, see below, p. 30.

Accordingly, we are at a loss to say whether the difference between having a house and having no house may be taken to describe the contrast between Baal and " the gods " literally or merely to symptomize it.

Similarly, we do not see exactly what is implied by the foregone conclusion that Baal could not possibly build a house for himself without first securing El's consent. In particular, we are unable to ascertain whether this applied to " the gods " as well—so that each of them had asked and was given El's permission to build—or whether it applied to Baal alone. In the former case, it is hard to understand why so much fuss and ado is made about the matter: why, instead of Baal's simply appealing to El himself, he should have to plot with Anat and Athirat and make them intercede in his behalf. In the latter case, we are left in the dark as to why Baal alone should have been discriminated against: by what offense, demerit, or overreaching ambition he might have incurred El's displeasure.

Especially perplexing is the position of El as it gradually emerges in the course of the epical development. His over-all authority is never questioned either by Baal or by Anat and Athirat, yet they are determined to make his authority serve their scheme even against his will and preference, indeed even by resorting to physical violence and short-lived deception. In terms of the epic, he is appealed to as the austere judge and benevolent father in whose power, and in whose power alone, it lies to grant his son the right to a house or to deny him that right. Yet it is assumed, at least by Anat, that he would be just as determined to turn a deaf ear to her intercession in behalf of his son. And when in the end he does yield to the plea of his gentle wife, it is apparently only because he was kept unaware of the true object of Baal's ambition—unaware that what Baal desired was not simply a house like that of any of " the gods," but an extraordinary house glittering with precious metals. It is indeed as if in the metallic character of Baal's future house, in his plan to have it built of gold and silver or, as he is once made to say, of " stone of splendor," we have to do with another motif of the building saga—a secondary and younger motif no doubt, but apparently no less acute and effective than the alliance-enmity motif.

The hazard of an exact appraisal is further enhanced by the extremely puzzling relationship between the two tablets that constitute our chief sources for the study of the building saga. Both tablets, designated in recent discussions as *2AB* and *5AB*, are badly broken up, the text being frequently interspersed with more or less hopeless lacunae. But to the extent to which the writing is preserved, it is clear that in 2AB the end of the text coincides with the end of a building narrative, the concluding lines relating how Baal informed Mot of the completion of the house.

A Scene of Baal's Wedding

It it just as clear that in *5AB*, from column 3 on, we have to do with the *beginning* of a narrative concerning Baal's building plan, while columns 1—2 may easily be understood as a preamble to that narrative. Although column 1 is broken both at the top and the bottom, enough of the text is intact to make us realize that we have here a description of a wedding feast, specifically, the wedding of Baal to his three brides. A personage referred to as the " servant " (*ʿbd*) and " attendant " (*sid*) of Baal is apparently in charge of the ceremony.[8]

[8] Accordingly, *sid* is not an imperative, as suggested by Virolleaud, but rather a participle (*sāʾid*); an imperative of the verb involved may be

He has just placed before the bridegroom a sumptuous meal (*ll.* 5-8) and now (*ll.* 9-26) he turns to the more important rites of the wedding feast: [8a]

1. ndd (9) y'šr w yšqynh (10)

2. ytn ks bdh (11)
3. krpn b klat ydh (12)
4. b krb 'ẓm ridn (13)
5. mt šmm

6. ks qdš (14) l tphnh aṯt
7. krpn (15) l t'n aṯrt
8. alp (16) kd yqḥ b xmr (17)
9. rbt ymsk b mskh (18)

10. qm ybd w yšr (19)
11. mṣltm bd n'm (20)
12. yšr ġzr ṭb ql (21)

13. 'l b'l b ṣrrt (22) ṣpn
14. ytmr b'l (23) bnth

15. y'n pdry (24) bt ar
16. apn ṭly (25) bt rb . . .

The interpretation of the above passage will be seen to hinge on the phrase *ks qdš l tphnh aṯt*, rendered by Virolleaud " la coupe sainte, puisse l'Épouse la voir," and the stichos *yšr ġzr ṭb ql*, which has been taken to form a couplet with the following stichos, whereby *ġzr*, often employed in Ugaritic as an epithet in the sense of

found in *2D* 5:20, *sad (sa'adī) kbd hmt*, "attend (or wait upon) and honor them," corresponding with the imperfect, *2D* 5:30, *tsad (tis'adu) tkbd hmt*, "she attends (or waits upon) and honors them"; on the plural suffix, referring to Hayin, see *UG*, 5.13 (Gordon renders here *sad* and *tsad* as "respect" and "she respected"; correctly in the Glossary, 586, "serve"), but cf. below, n. 28. It is tempting to combine Ugaritic *sad* with WS *sa'ad*, "to assist, to help, to refresh," by means of nourishment (Genesis 18:5); see Ges-Buhl, *s. v.*

[8a] See below, p. 22 (bottom); cf. n. 12.

" hero," or the like, would naturally refer to Baal.[9] In reality however, *ks qdš* appears to be used here in the technical sense of " cup of (matrimonial) dedication," if not indeed in the sense of " cup of betrothal," while in the following *l* we merely have a new instance of the particle *lā* employed for sentence negation.[10] Nor could *ġzr* possibly have been intended here as an epithet (*ġāzir?*) of Baal, since the agent of *yšr*, in both occurrences (*ll.* 10, 12), must be seen to be the same as in all the preceding verbs (*yʿšr*, *yšqynh*, etc.); namely, Baal's " servant " and " attendant." Consequently, *yšr ġzr ṭb ql* will have to be understood as forming a triplet with the two preceding stichoi, and the word *ġzr* recognized as representing an adverb (*ġazīr?*), in the sense of " aloud, powerfully." [11] The decisive point however is that, beginning with *ʿl bʿl*, the description of the narrator has apparently given way to a direct discourse constituting the wording of the song, specifically, of the wedding chant. The passage would thus read as follows:

1. He proceeds to felicitate him and bid him drink; [12]
2. He puts a cup in his hand,
3. A jar in both his hands,

---

[9] *PL*, p. 51: " The Hero, good of voice, sings. Baal goes up into the heights of Ṣapān." For the strophical arrangement, cf. Virolleaud, a. 1.

[10] Cf. Akkadian *qadištu*, " temple-prostitute "; Hebrew *qiddaš*, " to dedicate, to consecrate," Syriac *qaddeš*, " to give in marriage "; Mishnaic *qiddûš*, " betrothal "; see *Mish. Qidd.* 2 : 2, " be thou betrothed (*hitqaddĕši*) unto me by this cup of wine." For the stylistic device of describing the extraordinary as something no one has ever seen, or known, or heard about, cf. " Negation," pp. 237 f. and n. 10.

[11] Arabic *ġazīr*, " abundant," may be applied to water, rain, beneficence, knowledge and " any thing " (Lane).

[12] I believe that Ugaritic *ʿšr* should be combined with Hebrew *'šr*, which in the intensive (denominative) stem is used both in the sense of " to make happy " and in that of " to felicitate, to pronounce happy," that is, no doubt, to salute one by saying *'ašrê*, " Hail! " or " Happy! "—

4. With a rope strong (and) supple
5. Which he stretches out heavenward.[13]
6. (It's) a cup of betrothal no woman has ever seen,
7. A jar no goddess has ever beheld: [14]
8. A thousand pitchers it contains of wine,
9. A myriad are blended in its mixture.[15]
10. (Now) he rises to chant, and to sing,
11. With cymbals, a pleasant song;
12. He sings aloud, good in voice:
13. " Baal has come up to the Fastness of Ṣapon,

---

very much like Arabic *sallama*, Sem. *brk* (intensive). It is remarkable that, when the stichos before us is taken together with that of *l.* 10, we obtain a close parallel of the significant, and as yet unexplained, passage of *2D* 6 : 30 ff. Compared with the context of the scene before us, Anat would seem to offer Aqhat not only the prospect of eternal life but that of sexual happiness as well; cf. " Incubation," n. 30. Apparently the drinking, from the " cup," is here more essential a part of the ceremony than the eating; in Hebrew, we recall, the word *mištê*, literally " drinking," is used for " feast, celebration," also for a wedding (cf. Judges 14 : 10, 12).

[13] The couplet, possibly an overly long stichos (so Virolleaud), is highly problematic. Presumably, it describes a cultic or symbolic action concerning the " cup." Having put it in Baal's hands, the " servant " now winds around it, in spiral fashion (?), a " rope " (or " twig, reed "?), which he makes " extend " (*mt* = *mattō* < *mattahu*) skyward beyond the rim of the cup (cf. *haš-šāmaymâ* in Exodus 9 : 8, etc.). For the vocables, cf. Arabic *karab*, " rope "; *ru'd*, " [a branch, or twig] in the most fresh, or supple, and soft, or tender, state; in the first year of its growth "; *matta*, " to extend, to stretch out," a rope, etc. (Lane).

[14] As far as one can see, this is the first, but hardly the only, instance in which *atrt* may clearly be seen to be employed as an appellative, that is, as the female counterpart of *il* and *b'l* in the appellative sense of " god, deity "; cf. " Incubation," n. 30; hence, no doubt, the corresponding usage of *'ăšērâ* in Hebrew, e. g., Judges 3 : 7, " and they served the Baalim and the Asheroth,' that is, the foreign male and female gods; cf. the use of *ištaru* in Akkadian, e. g., *ilšu u ištaršu*, " his god and goddess " (Muss-Arnolt, *s. v.*).

[15] So, with *yqḥ* in the sense of *occupare* (the agent being *ks-krpn*), and with *ymsk* in the passive (referring to *rbt*, viz. *kd*, while the suffix in *mskh* would again refer to *ks-krpn*), perhaps more likely than the rendering of both verbs as active, so that their agent would be the " servant-attendant "; cf. Virolleaud, a. l., and *PL*, p. 51.

14. Baal will visit his lasses;[16]
15. He will behold Pidriya, daughter of Ar,
16. Even Ṭilliya, daughter of Rabb . . ."

At this point the writing of column 1 breaks off except for one or two words. Otherwise we would no doubt have met here with the third of Baal's "lasses," namely, Arṣiya, daughter of Ya'buddar.[17] Since, as we shall see, they are prominently mentioned in several crucial turns of the building saga, and are referred to by Baal as his "perfect brides," it is safe to surmise that in the missing conclusion of column 1, the narrator related how, following the marriage ceremony, Baal decided to build a house for himself and his wives. This decision, we must further realize, was prompted, not by considerations of domestic comfort, but rather as an expedient of safety: the future house was to avert the danger of his wives' being carried off by Baal's enemy or enemies. Indeed, a direct hint to that effect may be found in an utterance of Baal concerning his curious notion that the house should have no windows.[18] When, therefore, in column 2, the narrator undertakes to describe the furious warfare of Anat, it should be clear that in doing so he was

[16] I believe that *ytmr* represents a Gt stem (cf. *ytlk*) of a root *mrr* (Arabic *marra*, "to go on, to proceed") or *m-r* (Arabic *māra*, also *tamawwara*, "to move to and fro, to come and go"). It was the *bnth* of the passage before us that led scholars to the notion that we deal here with Baal's "daughters" and, accordingly, that *ar* and *rb* are epithets applied to Baal; as is well known, neither Arabic *banāt* nor Hebrew *bānôṯ* need mean "daughters" in the literal sense of the word; cf. Song of Songs 2:2, etc.

[17] See below, p. 31 f. and n. 35. Following *bt rb*, only two complete words are preserved of the remainder of column 1: *pdr yd'*, which is perhaps to be combined with Arabic *baḏara* (Hebrew *pzr*), "to strew, scatter about," and *mīda'*, "garment, sackcloth."

[18] *2AB* 6:8 ff.; is perhaps *mdd ilym* merely a more emphatic form (see below, n. 92) of *mdd ilm*, known to be employed as an epithet of Mot?

guided by the desire to explain etiologically why Baal chose Anat as his ally in the building plan which he was about to relate in column 3 and on to the end of the tablet.

A Problem of Source Criticism

The question thus arises as to the precise relationship of the two poems, both of which are wholly dedicated to the building epic. Are they part of one and the same narrative, so that *2AB* would represent the continuation or, at any rate, the conclusion of the story that began in *5AB*?[19] This assumption, we must recognize, is all but precluded by the realization that *5AB* describes the same three major episodes that are related in the early part of *2AB*; namely, (*a*) how Baal prepared to send an intercessor in his behalf to El, the intercessor being Anat in *5AB* and Athirat in *2AB*; (*b*) how, eventually, the intercession was carried out; and (*c*) how, as a result, Hayin was summoned to come to Baal. The difficulty might be somewhat mitigated by assuming that Anat had failed in her mission, and therefore a new attempt was made by Athirat.[20] But if so, the summons to Hayin would be premature and hence entirely out of place in *5AB*.

No difficulty at all would exist, however, if we were to assume that, in the two tablets before us, we deal, not with different parts of the same narrative, but with

[19] Virolleaud, Avant-propos, p. v: "Il paraît évident, non point dès l'abord, mais à la lecture des épisodes *E* et *F*, que *V AB* précédait immédiatement le poème *II AB*. . . ."

[20] Virolleaud, p. 89: "El n'a-t-il donc pas accueilli favorablement a requête de sa fille? On peut le penser, puisque Ašérat [that is, Athirat], épouse de El, devra plus tard intervenir à son tour, et que c'est à ce moment-là seulement que El dira enfin *hm . . . ybn bt l B'l.*"

two different narratives of the building saga—told by different narrators, no doubt in different communities or locales, and perhaps first committed to writing by different scribes. Insofar, therefore, as the two tablets cover the same ground—as exemplified in the three episodes just mentioned—they would be parallel rather than consecutive, the narrative of *5AB* having been continued on a tablet that has not been discovered by the excavators, while that of *2AB* had its antecedent in yet another undiscovered tablet. The matter would be clinched, of course, if it could be shown that, according to *5AB*, Anat did succeed in extorting from El his consent to Baal's request, thus superseding the parallel mission of Athirat as related in *2AB*. Unfortunately, however, the particular passage that told of El's reply to Anat is broken off the tablet, so that once again we seem to find ourselves in a blind alley.

Even more enigmatic is the relationship between our two main witnesses to the building epic, on the one hand, and the fragment of yet another witness to that epic, a text which has been designated as *6AB*, on the other. Although fully a third, if not half, of that text is missing altogether and, of the columns extant, hardly a single line appears to be complete, it is nevertheless clear that we have to do here with a poem related in substance to *5AB*, though no connection with *2AB* may be plainly discerned as far as the fragment goes.[21] Just

[21] If we restore *6AB* 3:27-29 (as we evidently should) to read *ḥš* [*rmm hkl-m*], *b tk* [*ṣrrt ṣpn, w*]*bn* [*bt ksp w xrṣ*], "Pray [raise a palace], In the midst [of the Fastness of Ṣapon, And] build [a house of silver and gold]," we do obtain a passage corresponding to *2AB* 4-5:113 ff. (cf. *2AB* 4-5:80, 95). This or a very similar restoration is suggested by the two passages being found in closely parallel scenes: In *2AB*, Baal invites Hayin to a banquet; when the master-builder arrives, and the meal is put before him, Baal bids him proceed with the building operations. In

as clearly it represents a building narrative that differed essentially from that told in *5AB* and, with varying details, in *2AB*. For here, in *6AB*, it is El and not Baal who appears to be the hero in search of an extraordinary kind of house who summons the master-builder Hayin to help him achieve his objective. Are we not therefore faced here with a rivalry between two schools of Ugaritic etiology—say between the priests of El and those of Baal—as to which of these two gods had inaugurated the age of metallurgy by appointing the Egyptian Hephaistos to build for him a house of precious metals?

New Material on the Building Saga

That, in the peculiar logic of folklore, a sufficiently vital motif may be exploited in a variety of moods and manners is amply well known from the epics of Sumer and Akkad, the myths of ancient Egypt, the popular narratives of the Hebrews, and the fables and legends of Greece as well as of more recent cultural milieus. It is therefore not at all surprising that the hero of the Ugaritic building saga should have been identified, now with Baal, now with El, or that the chief protagonist of the hero should have been represented, now by Anat, now again by Athirat. Nor need we assume that Ugaritic folklore concerning the intrigues and struggles

6AB, Baal is merely replaced by El, otherwise the scene is essentially the same: El had invited Hayin to visit him so that he might tell him about an important, unheard-of affair, "a monument" he very much desired (*6AB* 3:12-16)—exactly what we shall see Baal wished to convey and eventually did convey to Anat. It is therefore an all but inescapable inference (and admirably borne out by what is left in the passage: *ḥš . . . b tk . . . bn*) that when the master-builder arrives, El bids him here what, in *2AB*, he is bid by Baal (*ḥš . . . tbn . . . tk*); cf. further *bt kspy*, "my house of silver," *6AB* 4:21, also in an utterance of El, but addressed, it would seem, to Mot. See also below, n. 24.

among the gods or the advance of the age of metallurgy was confined to just the narrative patterns evidenced in the three epical poems which we have considered. In point of fact, a fragment recently published by Virolleaud [22] makes it highly probable that, had the tablet designated as *3AB* been preserved in entirety, we would have found it to be a version of the building saga on a par with that of *2AB*, *5AB*, and *6AB*. But even with our sketchy knowledge of the contents of this tablet, we cannot fail to see that it reflects a version widely at variance with any of those three poems, yet sharing with them in what we have been led to discern as the basic issues of Ugaritic mythology.

We recall how, in a fragment of *3AB*—Virolleaud's *A* fragment—Baal destroys an enemy named Prince Sea and Chieftain River by means of a " staff " or " rod," no doubt made of metal, which Hayin had " fashioned " for him for this purpose.[23] This strange episode, which

[22] In " Fragments mythologiques de Ras-Shamra ": " Le dieu 'Aštar (III *AB*, *C*)," *Syria 24* (1944-45), 1-12. I am indebted to my colleague Prof. A. Goetze for having placed at my disposal his copy of this issue—apparently the only copy available in this country to date.

[23] Previous translations of the remarkable scene (by Ginsberg, *The Ugarit Texts*, p. 75, in Hebrew; and Gordon, *PL*, pp. 51 ff.), while admirable on the whole, appear to have missed one or two of its salient features, mainly because of their unawareness of the negative force of the particle *l* in three successive clauses, but also, no doubt, because the testimony of the *C* fragment was not known at the time the translations were made. In particular, I understand the lengthy passage (*ll.* 11-28) to the effect that Hayin " fashions " (*ynḥt*) first only one " staff " or " rod " (*ṣmd-m*), but since its blows fail to affect Prince Sea, he makes another staff which does produce the desired results. Each time Hayin pronounces the staff's " design " or " destiny " (*śmth-m*), gives it a name (*šmk at*), and recites an invocation over it; within the invocation, all verbs and pronouns of the third person (excepting, of course, *yprsḥ* and *yql*) refer to Baal; see the Repertory, No. 18. Something of a puzzle has been the succinct reference to the goddess Athtart (*'ṯart*) immediately following the above scene. Obviously, then, this goddess, while not

expands the Hephaistos' qualification as a master-builder to include that of a maker of weapons—in agreement with his qualification as an artisan of fabulous bows referred to in the Daniel poem—but does not explain why Hayin should have stepped out of his role as Baal's architect to become his armorer as well, is now admirably elucidated by the new fragment, which has long since been recognized by Virolleaud as having formed a part of *3AB* and is designated by him as the *C* fragment of this tablet. Specifically, the fragment relates how Hayin is ordered by El to build a house, not for the supreme god himself, nor for Baal, but for none other than Prince Sea, Chieftain River. What is even more instructive, El's order to Hayin here parallels so closely Baal's corresponding commission to Hayin in *2AB* that, although the particular passage (*ll.* 6-10), as indeed the *C* fragment as a whole, is very badly preserved, it can in the main be restored with virtual certainty on the basis of that commission.[24]

figuring in the Ugaritic mythological texts hitherto available, must have been mentioned in *3AB* at a point or points that preceded the *A* fragment. (This is now made the more probable by the important part which, as will be seen presently, a god named Athtar plays in the building saga as reflected in the *C* fragment, so that Athtart may well have figured as his consort in the narrative of *3AB*.) At any rate, Athtart's "cry" (*tgʿr*) in *ll.* 28-30, *bṯ l aliyn bʿl . . . k šbyn zbl ym*, should be taken to mean "scatter him (or "disperse him," and the like; cf. Arabic *baṯṯa*), oh Aliyan Baal . . . for Prince Sea has made us captives" (implying that the latter had already invaded Mt. Ṣapon and that it is here where Hayin was to have built the house for him), with *bṯ* = *buṯṯū* < *buṯṯuhu* in agreement with *ybṯnn aliyn bʿl* in what immediately follows; cf. "Negation," n. 31.

[24] On the basis of the same commission (*2AB* 4-5 : 113 ff.), we have been led to restore El's order to Hayin in *6AB* (see above, n. 21) before being aware of the new parallel in *3AB* (C : 6-10) as restored by Virolleaud. The end of *l.* 6, left open by Virolleaud, should perhaps be restored to read [*gʿ*]*r y*[*gʿr il ḥš l*] *kṯr*, etc., in view of *tgʿr-m ʿṯtrt bṯ l aliyn bʿl* in *3AB* A : 28 (cf. above n. 23). To judge by the repeated

In short, we are dealing here with a Ugaritic narrative in which the antagonism between El and Baal lies much more on the surface—and in consequence, it would seem, the principal motifs appear more closely interwoven—than in either *2AB* or *5AB*: with El here openly scheming to divert Hayin's services from Baal; and with Hayin, in flagrant revolt against El, frustrating the scheme by utilizing his craftmanship to put into Baal's hands the weapon with which to destroy a " rival " of his building plan.

Partly by the explicit testimony of the new fragment, partly by its clear implications, we are in a position to discern several other peculiarities of the building saga as it was narrated in *3AB*. Supplementary details will no doubt be furnished by a third, as yet unpublished, fragment of the tablet, designated by Virolleaud as the *B* fragment. Subject to such supplementation, the narrative of *3AB* may be said to have been constructed along the following lines: (*a*) a son of El named Athtar appeals to his father to grant him the right to build a house for himself; (*b*) the deity commissioned to intercede with El in favor of the appeal is the sun-goddess Shapash; (*c*) when Athtar himself proceeds to El's residence—presumably in order to strengthen Shapash's intercession by his own plea—he hears his father urge Hayin to build a house for Prince Sea, Chieftain River; [25]

occurrence of *-k* in lines 11, 12, and 14, it would seem that the direct discourse of El, starting at the end of line 6, continues to the end of line 14. Unfortunately, the latter half of the passage involved (*ll.* 11-14) is so hopelessly distorted that nothing can be said as to its contents save that it includes a reference to 'Athtar (*l.* 12) and perhaps also one to Mot (*l.* 11).

[25] The abrupt transition in *C* from the narrator's description of someone journeying to El's residence (*ll.* 3-6) on the one hand, to the direct discourse of El's order to Hayin (*ll.* 6-10) on the other, suggests that

(*d*) he is then warned by Shapash that El would surely punish him, should he contest his father's decision;[25a] and (*e*) he complains bitterly about the wrong perpetrated by El against him, seeing that he is to remain without a house, while Hayin would be made to employ his craft for the benefit of Prince Sea, Chieftain River;[25b]

the journeying person (the agent of *ytn* in *l.* 4) is none other than Athtar: he arrives at his journey's end only to hear his father order the master-builder to erect a house for Prince Sea (cf. the preceding note). A dramatic coincidence of the same kind, indicated by similar abruptness of transition, seems to have been told by the narrator of *5AB* (*E* : 12-26).

[25a] *C* : 15-18. The phrase *l pn zbl ym ṣu*, "go forth to meet Prince Sea" (cf. below, n. 49) would seem to imply that, so far from accepting Shapash's intercession, El made the goddess convey to Athtar that he should show his respect and subordination toward Prince Sea by going out to meet him—presumably when he arrives at the topos of the house to be erected for him by Hayin, the topos being no doubt Mt. Ṣapon (see above, n. 23); it is not altogether certain, however, that *ṣu* is the word intended; in view of the immediately following lacuna, it might be part of such a word. The remainder of Shapash's statement, as far as it is preserved, is identical with a warning of the same goddess addressed to Mot (*1AB* 6 : 26-29); one cannot help suspecting that, in *al yšm'k ṯr il abk*, the verb involved is **śm'* rather than *šm'*; cf. the Ḥadith *yašma'i 'llāhu bihi*, "God will requite him for that"; Lane, *s. v. šama'a.*

[25b] *C* : 18-21. For [*l*]*qḥ by* in the sense of "he snatched me off, he thrust me away," or the like, cf. the connotations of Hebrew *lāqaḥ*, especially in the passive and the Nifal. It is tempting to analyze *lbum* as *l bu-m*, and to combine *bu* with Arabic *bī'ah* and *mabā'ah*, "abode, domicile, covert"; in this case *ard* would represent *r-d*, rather than *yrd*, and the phrase *l bu-m ard* would have a close counterpart in Arabic locutions like *rāda kala'an wa-manzilan*, "he looked for, sought after, herbage and an abode" (*LA 4*, 169; Lane, *s. v. rāda*); it would thus seem that in *b npšny* (*bi napšāniya*) we have a phrase identical in meaning with what elsewhere in Semitic (Hebrew, Aramaic) would be expressed by *bĕ* (or *min*) *napši*, "of my own accord," (the afformative *ān* serving merely as an element of emphasis?). There can be little doubt that, in line 20, *kṯrm* [. . .] should be restored to read *kṯr-m* [*w xss*]; hence, we would have in the preceding *trḥṣn* another instance of a grammatical plural, or dual, applied to Hayin (above, n. 8), less striking in the present context, since the master-builder is referred to here (also *l.* 7) by his double epithet "the Skillful and Discerning one"; like Arabic *raḥaḍa*, and Ethiopic *reḥeḍa*, Ugaritic *rḥṣ* would thus appear to be employed in the

(*f*) El, however, justifies his action on the ground that Athtar has no wife and therefore, we may supply, he is in no need of a house.[25c] Since in the end it is Baal and not Athtar who destroys El's protégé, as we have seen, the obvious implication is that his father's decision in favor of the latter not only wronged Athtar but imperiled Baal's cause as well and that, conversely, had El decided in favor of Athtar, Baal's own cause would have been well served.

From a mythological poem that does not, or at least does not directly, bear on the building saga, we learn that in Ugaritic folklore Athtar was held to be a favorite son of Athirat; as such, he was no doubt believed to be an ally of Baal, as was Athirat herself. At one point of the poem, he is, in fact, made to serve as Baal's alter ego. The poem relates how, following Baal's temporary death, El requested his spouse to name one of her sons who would be made Baal's successor; and how, after some deliberation, the goddess finally chose Athtar: him and none other did Athirat find to be worthy of occupying Baal's place, to reign over the Fastness of Ṣapon, to sit on the throne of Aliyan Baal.[26]

sense of "to sweat," as well as in that of "to wash (oneself)" and, by a well-known metonymy, here "to toil," etc.; cf. Latin *sudare*, *sudor*, and the locution "in the sweat of thy face shalt thou eat bread" (Genesis 3:9). For a connected translation of Athtar's dirge, in terms of the (tentative) observations just advanced, see the Repertory, No. 16.

[25c] *C*:21-24. It is tempting to suggest that the last three wedges in what Virolleaud transcribes as *a*(?)*n* represent, in reality, *a* and *t*, that is, *at*, "thou"; to judge by the autograph, the sign immediately preceding, now partly defaced, might very well have been *w* or *p*; thus the phrase would read *w*(*p?*) *at in aṯt* [*l*]*k k*[*m ilm*], "but thou—there is no wife [unto] thee lik[e (unto) the gods]," corresponding with *ank in* bt [*ly*] in line 19.

[26] *1AB* 1:45-65; one gains the impression that the deliberation (*ll.* 48-52) is merely a literary device designed to give Athtar's candidacy the force of emphatic finality. The fact that Athtar is given different epithets

We are thus led to wonder whether, in the narrative of *3AB*, we are not faced with a conniving maneuver of the kind we have encountered before: El is first made to believe that the house, the building of which he was asked to approve, was for Athtar; but after the maneuver has failed and El has rejected Athtar's plea, Baal resorts to the device of eliminating El's choice, thus establishing himself as the true petitioner behind his brother's appeal and, therefore, the true contestant of El's decision. We may also wonder whether El's reference to Athtar's unmarried status does not reflect a social tenet of the Ugaritic community whereby building a house for oneself was a necessary corollary to matrimony; and whether it was not with regard to such a tenet that the narrator of *5AB* related how Baal married his three brides before embarking upon his building campaign.

In the following sections an attempt has been made to examine in some detail a number of passages that seem to be of paramount importance for a reliable analysis of the building saga as told in *5AB*. Nearly all of these passages will be seen to bear on the phenomena which we have encountered; while their joint critical interpretation may well help to clarify the over-all picture of the building saga beyond the particular version of it reflected in one or another of the poetical narratives.

in the two poems—respectively, *ʿṯtr ʿrẓ* in *1AB*, and *ʿttr d tm(?) k[ḥ(?)]* in our fragment—should not prevent us from recognizing that we deal here with one and the same deity, as justly seen by Virolleaud; *Syria, 24*, 3. On **kḥ,* see below, p. 48.

"Grande Stèle (haut.: 1m42) du Ba'al au foudre."
From Claude F. A. Schaeffer, "Les Fouilles de Minet-el-Beida et de Ras Shamra" (*Syria*, 1933), Pl. XVI.

II. INVITATION TO AN ALLIANCE

Text and Translation

ON the tablet of *5AB*, the upper part of column 3, amounting to about two thirds of the entire column, is separated from the lower part by two horizontal strokes running across the full width of the column. This is a procedure sometimes employed by the Ugaritic scribes to indicate a new turn in the development of the narrative. As seen already by Virolleaud in his pioneer treatment of the text of *5AB*, the separating strokes are designed to mark off the end of a message to Anat from Baal, referred to here by his more formal name Aliyan Baal. Equally well marked is the beginning of the message: by the authentication "(Thus) spoke Aliyan Baal," a formula frequently occurring in the building narratives and in the Ugaritic epical poems in general. In addition to being thus clearly defined as to its beginning and end, the text of the message is unusually well preserved as to the legibility and continuity of its wording as well. Nevertheless, Virolleaud found himself obliged to remark that we deal here with a message "dont il n'est pas facile d'indiquer, d'un mot, la signification et la portée." Subsequent discussions, either of the message as a whole or of one or another of its parts, do not appear to have come any further in that respect.

The message represents only the concluding part of a direct discourse addressed by Baal to an envoy who was to take the message to Anat. Owing to a break at the head of the tablet, the beginning of Baal's charge to the envoy is missing. The break also deprives us of a reference as to the event or circumstance that had caused Baal to make the pronouncement that follows. Usually, such a reference is descriptive in nature, that is, given in the narrator's own words. The missing piece of clay, however, or rather a part of it, has been found by the excavators at Ras Shamra. It appears to contain the concluding lines of a scene, contained at the end of column 2, in which is described how Anat, following her massacre of a great number of persons—it is not clear whether human or divine—performs a thorough ablution. It is thus tempting to assume that, by way of a transition from that scene to the episode before us, the narrator told how, when word of Anat's mighty deeds had reached Baal on his mountain fastness, the Height of Ṣapon, following the god's wedding, he called for his attendant in chief, Gepen-and-Ugar, in order to dispatch him with a message to his victorious sister. At any rate, the lacuna at the beginning of the column that had been caused by the break at the head of the tablet—a lacuna which in the estimate of Virolleaud amounted to some twenty lines of text—will be seen to have comprised the three following items: (a) conclusion of the ablution scene; (*b*) transition to the present episode; (*c*) beginning of Baal's charge to his envoy.

From where the writing on the column is preserved to the end of the message, the text consists of twenty-eight lines of writing (*5AB* 3:1-28). Since these lines do not always coincide with the metrical stichoi, I have found it convenient, as on previous occasions, to mark the stichoi by numbers of their own, and to indicate the lines of writing by numbers in parentheses.[26a]

[26a] For the transliteration of the (clearly polyphonous) sign for *š* or *ś*, see "Negation," n. 3.

A *a*   — — — — — — — — — — —

        — — — — — — — — — — — —

        — — — (1) — — — — — — — —

1. [t]št rimt (2) 1 irth

2. mśr l dd aliyn (3) b'l
3. ṣd[q?] pdry bt ar (4)
4. ahbt ṭly bt rb
5. dd arṣy (5) bt y'bdr

b   6. km ġlmm (6) w 'rbn [27]
7. l p'n 'nt hbr (7) w ql
8. tštḥwy kbd hyt (8)

9. w rgm l btlt 'nt (9)
10. ṯny l ymmt limm (10)

B   11. tḥm aliyn b'l
12. hwt (11) aliy qrdm

a   13. qryy b arṣ (12) mlḥmt
14. št b 'prt ddym (13) [27a]

15. sk šlm l kbd arṣ (14)
16. arb dd l kbd šdm (15)

b   17. ḥšk 'ṣk
18. 'bṣk (16) 'my

19. p'nk tlsmn 'my (17)
20. tktḥ išdk dm [27b]

c   21. rgm (18) iṯ ly w argmk (19) [27c]
22. hwt w aṯnyk

---

[27] The first two signs of *'rbn* are partly defaced, but the reading is as good as certain.
[27a] Var. (in *5AB*): *b'pr-m*.
[27b] So, *tktḥ*, in *6AB*; Virolleaud (but hardly Tablet) here: *twtḥ*; cf. "Negation," n. 18.
[27c] Var. (in *5AB*): *w argmn*.

23. rgm (20) ‘ṣ
24. w lxšt abn (21)

25. tant šmm ‘m arṣ (22)[27d]
26. thmt ‘mn kbkbm (23)

27. abn brq dl td‘ šmm (24)
28. rgm l td‘ nšm
29. wl tbn (25) hmlt arṣ

30. at-m w ank (26) ibġyh[27e]
31. btk ġry il ṣpn (27)

32. b qdš b ġr nḥlty (28)
33. b n‘m b gb‘ tliyt

The division indicated above by the letters on the margin will be seen to be based on the contents of the discourse. As has been said already, Baal's statement consists in the main of (*A*) his charge to the envoy and (B) a message he desires to be delivered by the envoy to Anat. In turn, (*A*) is clearly divided into two parts. Although part *a* is broken up at the beginning, it seems safe to infer, as scholars have, that in it Baal ordered the messenger to present Anat with some sort of a gift of jewelry, while in part *b* he gives the envoy the usual directions about the manner in which the goddess should be approached.

Apart from the conventional authentication formula (*ll.* 11-12), the message proper (*B*) may be seen to be divided into three sections. Baal tells his sister that (*a*) she should carry on her warfare to the finish; that (*b*) she should hasten to visit him; and that (*c*) he wishes to speak to her about a matter of very great importance. In metrical and strophical respect the passage exhibits the characteristics normal in Ugaritic prosody. With the

[27d] Var. (in *6AB*): *tunt.*

[27e] Var. (in *6AB*): *at.*

possible exception of two, or four, lines (17-18 and 23-24), all stichoi of the discourse may be understood as following the three-stress pattern. Strophically, the passage would seem to be made up mostly of couplets, two triplets, and one quatrain; in one or two instances, it is possible that what looks like a pair of couplets was intended as a quatrain. However, with the major division secured by the analysis of the contents, the less vital subdivision into strophes or stanzas hardly bears on the undertanding of the passage and has therefore been left unmarked in the following translation.

A *a* --- --- --- ---

--- --- --- ---

--- (1) -------

1. Ye [shall] put a gem on her breast:
2. As a token of the love of Aliyan Baal,
3. Of the loyal[ty](?) of Pidriya, daughter of Ar,
4. Of the devotion of Ṭilliya, daughter of Rabb,
5. Of the love of Arṣiya, daughter of Ya'buddar.

b 6. Like stewards then do ye enter:
7. At the feet of Anat crouch ye and fall down,
8. Prostrate yourselves and honor her.
9. And proclaim ye to the Virgin Anat,
10. Declare to the Yamamat of the People:

B 11. "(Thus) spoke Aliyan Baal,
12. (Thus) said Aliy Qardam:
a 13. 'Strike thou the warriors to the ground,
14. Put to the dust the repellers,
15. Pour out submission to the core of the earth,
16. Overwhelm insurrection to the core of the land.

b 17. Let thy compassion (for me) constrain thee:
18. Let it unite thee with me.
19. Thy feet shall gallop toward me,
20. Thy tread shall stamp out impudence.

c 21. I have (at heart) a thing I wish to tell thee,
22. A matter I wish to convey to thee.
23. (It's) a thing about wood,
24. And a secret about stone.
25. (It's) the contention of heaven with the earth,
26. Of the deep with the stars.
27. (It's) stone of splendor, which the heavens have not known,
28. A thing that men have not known,
29. And the multitudes of the earth have not perceived.
30. (It concerns) a monument that I do desire,
31. Amid the mountain of mine, God of Ṣapon,
32. In Holiness, on the mount of my inheritance,
33. In Delight, on the hill of Endeavor.' "

In terms of the foregoing rendering, Baal's message will be seen at first sight to bear, directly or indirectly, on nearly all of the problems which we have encountered at the outset of the present study. In the following comments, however, it will be convenient to consider the individual sections of the discourse seriatim.

Aa. A Gift from Baal and His Brides (*ll.* 1-5). The initial word is rendered by Virolleaud *m* (?) *št* and left untranslated. On the photograph of the tablet, however, the first sign that is fairly discernible looks like that of *t*, and is preceded by an exceedingly faint wedge which might well be the remnant of *š*. By the evidence of the photograph, therefore, we would surmise that the word before us is *št*, and that we have here to do with an imperative in agreement with the series of imperatives in *Ab* (*ll.* 6-10). If *št* should in reality represent only part of the word on the tablet, as suggested by Virolleaud, it would seem much more probable to restore it to read [*t*]*št* than to follow his *m(?)št*. In *tšt* we would simply have an imperfect in the sense of an imperative, in agreement with the one instance of an imperfect in *Ab*.

Accumulative evidence, offered by our narrative as well as other Ugaritic texts, suggests that whether the word is *št* or *tšt* we should see in it, not a singular, *šīt*, "put thou," or *tašīt*, "thou shalt put," but rather a plural, *šītū*, "put ye," or *tašītū*, "ye shall put," if not indeed a dual (*šītā* or *tašītā*). The same applies to all other references—verbs, nouns, pronouns—to Baal's envoy. The plural designation would merely indicate that while Gepen-and-Ugar was Baal's chief spokesman, he was accompanied in his mission to Anat, also no doubt to other gods, by a number of lesser dignitaries or by a retinue of his own. Similarly, if a dual designation was intended it would suggest that Baal's spokesman was accompanied by a single attendant only. It is barely possible, however, and this was ably argued by H. L. Ginsberg, that Baal's missions to the gods were carried out by a pair of his ambassadors, one called Gepen and the other Ugar.[28]

[28] *BASOR*, *95* (1944), 25 ff. The evidence in favor of a dual interpretation is quite clear in *2AB*; in *5AB*, on the other hand, the pertinent references might well be plurals. If we take the position, as I believe we should, that Gepen-and-Ugar is the name of Baal's chief steward, and that the duals and plurals merely point to the attendant or attendants accompanying him on his missions in behalf of Baal (a situation no doubt derived from prevailing diplomatic etiquette), it would be conceivable that we have here one of the many points of detail in which the narrative of *2AB* deviates from that of *5AB*. Cf. the "three men" of Genesis 18:1, to whom reference is made now in plurals (*vv.* 5, 9), now in singulars (*v.* 10), and "the two angels" of Genesis 19:1; also the

Be this as it may, Baal charges his envoy or envoys to place on Anat's breast an object or objects called *rimt*—a feminine noun that might be either singular or plural. The word has been combined with Hebrew *rāmôṯ*, usually translated " corals," mentioned in Ezekiel 27 : 16 among the foreign wares imported by Tyre. In Arabic, the word *ra'mah*, literally " love, affection," is used of a bead or gem worn as an amulet and believed to be a cause of love or affection. Some such sense would seem to fit in our context and is perhaps the primary meaning of the biblical *rāmôṯ* as well. If our *rimt* is to be placed on Anat's breast as a " token " of Baal's love, the phrase would be oddly reminiscent of " set me as a seal upon thy heart " in Song of Songs 8 : 6.

The rendering " token " is based on the conjecture that *mśr* (*maśār?*) is identical in meaning and derivation with Arabic *mušīr*, " a sign, a hint, an indication," so that it would form a second accusative of *tšt*, qualifying *rimt*, while the following *l* would plainly be used here in the sense of Arabic *ilā*.[29] Of the four substantives that in turn qualify *mśr*, the word read by Virolleaud as *yd* is extremely doubtful. On the photograph, the sign preceding *d* is blurred, while its outline might be that of *ṣ* no less than that of *y*. Following *d*, a sign was ap-

coupling of Moses and Aaron, of Moses and Joshua (" his minister," Exodus 24 : 13), of Moses, Aaron and Hur (Exodus 17 : 10), of Elijah and Elisha (1 Kings 19 : 19 ff.; 2 Kings 2). In *2AB*, Athirat is accompanied, on her journey to El at Baal's behest, by Qaddish-and-Amrar and Anat; from the Keret narrative we learn of " two messengers " (*mlakm*) carrying out a mission on behalf of King Pbl. In all these instances, it is a natural assumption that, even where the references represent grammatical duals or plurals, only one envoy is understood as actually speaking. It is especially noteworthy that, occasionally (above, n. 8), Hayin may be found to be referred to by a plural, or dual, pronoun; see below, n. 78.

[29] In the sense just adduced, Arabic employs *'išārah* more frequently than *mušīr*, both vocables being constructed with *'ilā*.

parently defaced on the tablet, and the space has not been accounted for by Virolleaud, except that he has placed here a question mark. I venture to propose that the word intended is *ṣd*[*q*], that is, "loyalty," corresponding to the usage of *ṣidq* elsewhere in Semitic.[30]

At first sight the series *dd-ṣdq-ahbt-dd* is extremely puzzling. Specifically we fail to detect a syntactic element by which to connect the two opening stichoi (lines 1-2) with the three following ones (lines 3-5). The matter becomes clear enough, however, upon the observation that, in keeping with its great liking for appositives and asyndeton, Ugaritic is capable of employing the force of a single particle for a series of objects, in contrast to conventional Semitic syntax whereby the particle would be repeated before each member of the series. A particularly noticeable example is offered by Baal's "complaint" to which we have already referred (and are presently to refer in full):

Woe, there is no house unto Baal like (unto) the gods,
(Nor) a court like (unto) the sons of Athirat,

where apart from "no" being made to refer both to "house" and "court" (and this, despite the asyndeton),[31] a series of three objects is made to depend on a single preposition, namely the preposition "unto." Accordingly, we are led to realize, the phrase *mšr l*, or rather the preposition *l*, refers not only to *dd aliyn bʿl* but to the entire series before us. That is to say, the "gem" to be placed on Anat's breast was to serve as

[30] Cf. the use of *ṣdq* in the Zinjirli inscriptions (Panammu 19, Bar Rakab 4 f.); also in the Keret narrative (*1K* 1:12 f.): *aṯt ṣdqh*, "his loyal wife," paralleled with *mtrxt yšrh*, "his faithful spouse" (against Ginsberg, *LK*, p. 14).

[31] Asyndeton, *ḥẓr*, in *5AB* (E:47); in *2AB* (4-5:51): *w ḥẓr*; cf. the following note.

a token of—literally "to"—both the love of Aliyan Baal and the loyalty of Pidriya, etc.

It is most fortunate that at the outset of our tablet, in a scene describing Baal's wedding, we have met with two of the three personages referred to in the present section in addition to Baal and Anat; but for the break at the bottom of the tablet, we would almost certainly have met them all. For thus we understand why Baal here instructs his envoy to assure Anat not only of his own affection but also of that of his wives: in helping Baal's plan, the goddess would *ipso facto* be instrumental in securing their welfare as well. What is more important, we now understand the hitherto puzzling wording of Baal's "complaint" to El:

1. wn in bt l bʿl km ilm
2. w ḥẓr k bn aṯrt
3. mṯb il mẓll bnh
4. mṯb rbt aṯrt ym

5. mṯb klt knyt
6. mṯb pdry bt ar
7. mẓll ṭly bt rb
8. mṯb arṣy bt yʿbdr

Specifically, we may now see in this wording a highly effective device by which Baal undertakes to impress his father with the logic and justice of his plea:

1. Woe, there is no house unto Baal like (unto) the gods,
2. (Nor) a court like (unto) the sons of Athirat:
3. (Like) the dwelling of El that shelters his sons,
4. (Like) the dwelling of Lady Athirat of the Sea!
5. (No) dwelling for (his) perfect brides:
6. A dwelling for Pidriya, daughter of Ar,

7. A shelter for Ṭilliya, daughter of Rabb,
8. A dwelling for Arṣiya, daughter of Ya'buddar![32]

And we may further understand why, in urging Hayin to provide no windows for his future house, Baal should once again support his argument by referring to his wives.[33] In short, Baal's charge to the envoy he is about to dispatch to Anat, the wording of his "complaint" to El, and his argument with Hayin become coherent and consistent only in the light of the preamble of columns 1-2 of *5AB*; conversely, it is by these utterances of Baal that the preamble may in turn be seen to be as significant as it is ingenious.

It is not clear, however, whether the "daughter" qualifying each of Baal's brides should be taken literally, so that each of the following names would be that of the father of the particular "bride," or whether "daughter" here forms part of some sort of a *kunya*. Nor can anything be said with certainty about the meaning and the pronunciation of the names, beyond the fact that feminine nouns ending in *y*, both appellatives and proper names, are not unknown elsewhere in Semitic.[34] If *y'bdr* really represents such a name as Ya'buddar or Ya'biddar, we would have here one of the few instances in Uga-

[32] *2AB* 4-5 : 50 ff; see above, n. 5; in *5AB E*, the stichos *mṯb klt knyt* is made to follow, rather than to precede, our *ll.* 6-8, which would make the plea especially impressive. In terms of the above rendering of the passage, the force of *k(m)*, in *ll.* 1-2, extends to *ll.* 3-4, while that of *in* not only extends to the immediately following stichos, *l.* 2, but is resumed in the new quatrain as a whole or even, perhaps, in each stichos of the quatrain (*ll.* 5-8). For the rendering "for," cf. "Incubation," p. 11 (on *il-m dnil*). Of the two occurrences of *mẓll*, I understand the first as a participle (*maẓallil*) and the second as a nomen loci.

[33] See above, n. 18, cf. also p. 20, and n. 25c.

[34] Cf. the name *śry*, probably the older form of *Sarah* (Genesis 17 : 15), and see Nöldeke, *ZDMG*, *40*, 183, and *42*, 484; for Ugaritic, see *UG*, 7.27.

ritic folklore of a proper name involving a verbal form in the imperfect tense: "May-he-act (or serve) -continually."[35] The reference to Baal's consorts in the present connection should have precluded the curious suggestion that his message to Anat is to be understood as something like a proposal of marriage—a suggestion to which we shall have to refer repeatedly in the course of the present discussion.

Ab. Homage to a Goddess (*ll.* 6-10). Except for three details that stand in need of clarification, the unit before us is as lucid as could be desired. In it, Baal tells his envoy that he and his companion or companions should enter into the presence of Anat in the manner becoming to stewards (*ġlmm*), rather than in that of visitors calling upon an equal, let alone an inferior (*l.* 6); and that, accordingly, they should humble themselves at the feet of the goddess in prostration and reverence (*ll.* 7-8) before addressing themselves to her (*ll.* 9-10). The phrasing is familiar to us from its frequent occurrence in similar scenes, both in descriptive passages and, as in the instance before us, in direct discourse. In short, we have here to do with a case of parallel passages having reference to a standard situation: appearance before a major deity. The three details that have not been made sufficiently clear concern (1) the nature of the word *ʿrbn*, (2) the function of the *w* preceding it, and (3) the meaning of the epithet *ymmt limm*.

[35] In a proper name, it would not be unnatural if *yʿbd dr* was contracted to *yʿbdr*; in the Ugaritic poems other proper names representing imperfects might be *yman* (*2AB* 1:43) and *yṭpn* (*1D*:214, etc.); possibly, but not probably, also *yṣb*; see *LK*, p. 6 (but cf. "Negation," n. 21); in the Ugaritic community, proper names of this type do not seem to have been particularly rare; cf. *RA*, *37* (1940), *passim*.

There can be no question whatsoever that *'rbn* must be seen to be a verb form in the nature of a command, in agreement with the six other verbs of our passage, of which five are imperatives, plain and simple, and one is an imperfect in the sense of an imperative. This was properly seen by Virolleaud, but he did not offer to analyze the particular morphology involved, which appears to have greatly puzzled subsequent scholars.[36] In reality, however, we can hardly fail to recognize in the final *n* a strengthening element. The question can only be whether we have here to do with an energetic imperative, as employed in Arabic, or—and this is much more likely—with a syntactic device best known to us from Hebrew. It is the device whereby an imperative, a cohortative, or a jussive (Genesis 26:28: *tĕhî nâ*; 2 Samuel 19:38: *yāšoḇ-nâ*) may be modified by the enclitic particle *na*, a particle of entreaty, of encouragement, of persuasion, of urgency. Accordingly, *'rbn* should be understood as *'rb-n*, that is *'urubū/ā-na* or *'iribū/ā-na*, " do enter, pray enter," or the like. It has long been noted that the particle *na* appears to be employed in the Amarna letters for approximately the same function as in Hebrew, which would greatly strengthen the assumption of its presence in Ugaritic as well.[37]

[36] It is taken by Albright, *BASOR, 70,* 19 (and n. 5), to be a noun, " pledged slave "; Goetze, *JBL, 60,* 355, renders *'rbn* as " had entered," again without accounting for the form of the vocable; Gordon, *PL,* p. 54, leaves the word untranslated; both he and Ginsberg (*BASOR, 95,* 26, n. 1) appear to doubt the reading (without sufficient ground, I believe; see above, n. 27).

[37] Böhl, *Die Sprache der Amarnabriefe,* p. 1 74 (Leipziger Semitische Studien 5, 2); Ebeling, *Das Verbum der Amarna Briefe,* pp. 69 ff. (Beiträge zur Assyriologie 8, 2). The presence of the enclitic *na* would add to the already considerable orthographic ambiguity of Ugaritic verbs with *-n*—especialy of *yqtln* and *tqtln,* in which the suffix may represent

I have long felt, and so apparently have others, that the sole problem of the *w* preceding *ʿrbn* is one of position; and that, in other words, *km ġlmm w ʿrbn* is only another way of saying *w km ġlmm ʿrbn*. But the matter hardly ends here. Great freedom in the word order of verbal clauses, it is true, forms an outstanding characteristic of Ugaritic, especially no doubt in the epical style of the narratives. It is very possible, however, that the construction in question involves an adverbial function of *w*—comparable to Arabic *fa*, "so, then, thus, that"—rather than the purely copulative sense. If so, our stichos could not be replaced by *w km ġlmm ʿrbn*, any more than it could be replaced by *w ʿrbn km ġlmm*, without thereby undergoing a change in meaning or, at least, in the shade of meaning. In short, it is quite conceivable that even if the stichos were introduced by a copulative *w*, it would still have retained its present construction: *w km ġlmm w ʿrb-n*. One need only compare the Arabic sentence pattern *allāha fa-ʿbud*, "Allah then do thou serve" (Koran 39:66) on the one hand,

either a pronominal object, or the energicus afformative, or else the flectional ending of the masc.-fem. plural, *(ū)n*, or dual, *ān*, or of the fem. second person singular, *īn*—whenever the context might imply a jussive or cohortative mood; at the same time, however, it would reduce the number of instances which hitherto could only be understood as representing a purely arbitrary and inconsistent usage of the moods, especially of the energicus; see "Negation," n. 34, and below, notes 59, 78, 93. The suggestion advanced by Gordon (*UG*, p. 51, n. 2) that the Hebrew particle *na* is a survival of the energicus is hardly admissible, seeing that the energicus afformative invariably *precedes* an object suffix, while *na* is just as invariably made to *follow* such a suffix; moreover, *na* may be found to strengthen vocables other than verbs (e. g., *'al, hinnê, 'im*). That, of the series of imperatives before us, only the first (*ʿrb*) should have been reinforced by *na* is in keeping with the use of the particle in Hebrew (cf. *śâ nâ ʿênêḵâ û-rĕʾê*, Genesis 13:14; *'êlĕḵâ nâ wa-'ăšallēm*, 2 Samuel 15:17; etc.), while repetition of the particle is extremely rare (cf. Judges 16:28).

and the pattern *wa-'ilā rabbika fa-rġab*, "and towards thy Lord then do thou strive" (Koran 94:8) on the other. The phenomenon will interest us again presently.[38]

Anat is here—and here only—given the epithet *ymmt limm*, which has been generally taken to be assimilated from *ybmt limm*, the latter form occurring regularly in the Ugaritic poems as an epithet of Anat. This is a very natural assumption, except that nothing plausible may be said as to why the goddess should have borne the awkward nickname "the *ybmt* (that is, presumably, "The-Widowed-Sister-in-Law") of Nations." Might not, therefore, *ybmt* represent a form dissimilated from, rather than assimilated to, *ymmt*, so that our passage would have preserved the original form of the epithet? In this case, we would perhaps be dealing here with a noun identical with the name or epithet of the renowned seeress of Arabic folklore—a blue-eyed lass who is said to have had such piercing sight that she could detect an army thirty miles away, and to whom it is believed

[38] See Reckendorf, *Arabische Syntax*, p. 316, and the examples, pp. 318 ff.; also Brockelmann, *Grundriss*, *2*, 442 f. (who, however, leaves the particle untranslated and who, moreover, adduces material from Hebrew that would require a different analysis). A close counterpart of the use of *w* in our stichos is offered in the Nikkal poem (see Goetze, *JBL*, *60* (1941), 353 ff.): *nkl w ibd ašr*, "of Nikkal, then, I chant, I sing"; thus the difficulties pointed out by Ginsberg (*BASOR*, *95*, 26, n. 6) are purely imaginary, since the *w* here does not mean "and." On the other hand, the case of *mra w tk pnh* (*2AB* 4-5:107) merely exhibits the positional freedom of the conjunction, the phrase standing in lieu of *w mra tk pnh*. The phenomenon, however, should not be confused with sentences like *b nši ʽnh w tphn* (against Goetze, *op. cit.*, n. 21), "when she lifted her eyes, she perceived him"; for here we simply have a temporal clause, with the conjunction introducing the main clause (cf. "Incubation," p. 20*b* and n. 44). For other instances of what from the point of view of conventional syntax might be called a displaced *w*, see below on *l*. 30 of the passage under discussion.

the district al-Yamāma, in Central Arabia, owes its name.[39]

B. Authentication Formula (*ll.* 11-12). Again we come upon a stereotyped locution applied to a standard situation: authentication of the sender of a message and of its wording. With one noticeable exception, to be considered later on, the formula recurs invariably in the Ugaritic texts whenever a message is ordered to be delivered verbatim; also, when, in due time, it actually is so delivered. In the several instances in which the sender of the message is Baal, the formula employed is identical with our couplet in every detail. Unfortunately, nothing can be said with certainty as to the meaning of *aliyn*, *aliy*, *qrdm*, or as to what the exact relationship between *aliyn* and *aliy* is.[40]

Without sufficient reason, I believe, scholars have treated the two appellatives of the couplet, *tḥm* and *hwt*, as nouns. In reality, all that may be said is that, outside this formula, two vocables written in the same manner as those before us do appear to be used as substantives, certainly *hwt*, probably also *tḥm*. However, in view of *rgm*, which is employed in Ugaritic now as a verb, now as a noun, and of similar instances where words, in consonantal writing, may be so employed in Semitic elsewhere (*dbr*, *'mr*, *xbr*, etc.), we should at least consider it possible that *tḥm* and *hwt* were also so employed. Offhand, it should be much more fitting for the transmitter of an *oral* message to begin with

[39] See Nicholson, *A Literary History of the Arabs*, p. 25, and *EI*, "Al-Yamāma." Albright has long since suggested that *ybmt* might be dissimilated from *ymmt* (*BASOR*, *70*, 19 n. 6), but he renders the word "progenitress," on grounds admittedly problematic; cf. Ginsberg, *BASOR*, *97*, 8 f. (who provisionally proposes to render *ybmt* as "the lass").

[40] Cf. *JAOS*, *56* (1936), 497, and below, n. 92.

" Thus says N. N."—for which numerous examples could be cited from nearly every branch of Semitic literature—than with " Message of N. N." With *hwt* taken as a verb, we would have a Ugaritic equivalent of the Hebrew root underlying the *hap. leg.* of Psalms 62:4 (*tĕhôṯĕṯû*) and of the dialectical Arabic *hawwata*, " to call, to shout," while *tḥm* might possibly—despite the velar *x* in Akkadian and Arabic—be identical with Aramaic *taḥḥem*, used in Syriac in the sense of " to define, to forbid, to appoint." Moreover, in the one noticeable deviation from the formula to which we have just referred, *tḥm* actually appears to be employed as a verb, with the pronominal *k* as its direct object.[41]

Ba. Purging of Enemies (*ll.* 13-16). We thus come to the message proper, or rather to the first part of the message. As is the norm in the Ugaritic epical texts, the whole message, including the authentication formula (lines 11-12), is repeated verbatim—although not, of course, without some scribal variants—when the narrative has advanced to the point of relating how Baal's envoy accomplished his mission and did deliver the message to Anat (D:51-64). Moreover, except that the imperatives are replaced by imperfects of the first

[41] See below, pp. 79 f. and n. 90. It is remarkable, at any rate, that *tḥm* seems to be employed exclusively in connection with delivery of a message. Since in antiquity a written record was believed to embody the spoken word, it would be natural if, with an ever-growing custom of delivering messages in writing, a noun derived from *tḥm* should have come to be used in the sense of " (written) message." On Arabic *hawwata*, cf. *Tāj al-'Arūs* (Cairo, 1898-90), *1*, 597 (*wa-hawwata bihi tahwītan ṣāḥa . . . yuhawwitu 'ai yunādī*); *Qamūs* (Bulak, 1289) *1*, 189 (*wahawwata bihi . . . ṣāḥa wa-da'āhu*). Following a suggestion by D. H. Baneth (*OLZ*, 1932, p. 451), Ugaritic *hwt* has been combined with Akkadian *awātu*; we shall see, however (below, p. 50), that this vocable appears to have the same equivalent in Ugaritic as elsewhere in WS.

person singular, the first part of the message is rephrased twice again in Anat's reply to Baal's envoy (D:66-69; 72-75), which admirably confirms the impression that in *Ba* we have to do with a contextually independent part of the message. It is especially noteworthy that, in *6AB*, the first two parts of Baal's message, *Ba* and *Bb*, form a message to Anat from El (2:18-23).

As suggested by the translation of *Ba* given above, Baal here advises his sister in effect that she should purge the land of " warriors " and " repellers " until universal submission has been made complete. The notion that Baal here proposes to outlaw war and to have Anat establish "peace on earth," would seem untenable on grounds a priori. Rather, we are all but compelled to realize that the " warriors " and " repellers " can refer only to Baal's enemies and adversaries, whether acute and actual or latent and potential. Thus the matter related in our tablet in what immediately precedes the present scene, that is in columns 1-2, would again prove a curiously fitting preamble to the main subject of the tablet. Baal here would merely suggest to Anat that she continue her ruthless warfare; except that in doing so, the message implies, she would now be serving the cause of Baal. We shall see, too, that Anat's reactions, first, at the mere appearance of Baal's envoy and, second, after the message had been delivered to her, bear out the above understanding of the passage. For the present, it may therefore suffice to consider the several details involved.

Morphologically, the word *qryy* is extremely difficult. Since the verb, like the parallel verbs in what immediately follows (*št*, *sk*), is obviously an imperative, we would expect it to be written *qry*—in keeping with *rgm*

|| *ṯny* in what precedes. The simplest explanation would be that the final *y* is a mater lectionis: a device employed by the scribe to prevent the reader from mistaking it for a perfect referring to Baal: " he has stricken," etc., a mistake which would have been enhanced by the preceding perfects in " thus spoke Aliyan Baal," etc. If so, *qryy* would simply stand for *qry* (presumably *qarriyî*).[42]

Semantically, *qryy* becomes clear in combination with its Hebrew equivalent *qārâ*, " to encounter, to come upon, to befall," and the Hebrew synonyms *pāgaš* and *pāgaʿ*, all of which verbs may be found used in a hostile sense: " to strike, to fall upon, to attack." Some such sense, moreover, is evidenced in another occurrence of the verb in Ugaritic itself and, as it happens, in a direct discourse of Anat. We notice, too, that in the sense of " strike," *qryy* forms a logical parallelism with *št b ʿprt* (var. *ʿpr-m*), " put to the dust." [43]

[42] For other instances of vocalic representation in Ugaritic (after consonants other than '), see *UG*, 3.5, also " Incubation," pp. 25 f. Such scholars as did recognize that *qryy* must be taken to represent a demand have been led to see in the final *y* a pronominal suffix (Virolleaud, hesitatingly, also Dussaud, Aistleitner) or to consider the form as an absolute infinitive, in *-ē*, with the force of an imperative (Goetze, *BASOR*, *93*, 18, and n. 12); see the following note.

[43] Cf. 2D 6 : 43-45, which I venture to submit should be restored and translated thus: *l aqryk b ntb pšʿ*, [*hn*] *b ntb gan ašqlk, tḥt* [*nxt ir*] *tk, nʿmn ʿmq nšm*, " I shall surely strike thee in [thy] rebellious path; [Lo,] in [thy] proud path I shall humble thee. There shall come down thy [repose of hea]rt, Naaman, astutest of men! " (whereby *tḥt* would be a feminine imperfect of *nḥt*; for the locution, cf. Isaiah 2 : 17; Daniel 5 : 22; for different treatments of the passage, cf. Albright, *BASOR*, *94*, 34: Ginsberg, *BASOR*, 98, 28). Because of the as yet unclear context, it would be hazardous at present to determine the exact meaning of *tqry* (Virolleaud: " elle rencontre " ou " tu rencontreras "), in *5AB* B : 4. In previous discussions, our *qryy* has been rendered " viens me trouver " (Virolleaud), " offre moi " (Dussaud), " setz mir " (Aistleitner), " remove (Goetze), " who meet me " (Albright), " dépose " (Herdner). See below, n. 55.

There can be little doubt that in *mlḥmt* we have to do with a plural of *mlḥm* (*malaḥḥim?*) or else of *mlḥmt*. The use of feminine plurals of masculine nouns is not uncommon in Arabic (e. g., *al-muhāgirah*, " the flight companions," of Muhammad); quite frequent, too, is the strengthening of an adjectival noun by means of a feminine ending: *xalīfah*, " Calif," *'allāmah*, " very learned." Nor is this an isolated instance in Ugaritic. Elsewhere in our narrative, the masculine word for " enemy " is paralleled with the feminine form *ṣrt*, " rival " or " rivals." Conversely, the feminine *mlḥmt* is here paralleled with the masculine *ddym*. I take it that the singular *ddy* represents a relative adjective from an abstract or verbal substantive *dd*, which is used in the final stichos of *Ba* (*l.* 16); and that the root of *dd* is *ḏ-d*, used in Arabic in the sense of " to drive away, to debar, to repel," by means of physical resistance; hence the nomen instrumenti *miḏwād* came to mean " the horn " of a bull, or " a spear "; for example " the bull repels (*yaḏūd*) from himself with his horn (*bi-miḏwādihi*) ."[44]

In the phrase *sk šlm*, it is natural to see in *sk* an imperative of *nsk*, " to pour, to pour out," frequently employed in the figurative sense of " spreading, radiating," and the like. In the same sense, such objects as " wrath " or " contempt " are said in Hebrew to be " poured out " upon someone or something. It is also natural to recognize in *šlm* the Semitic word for " peace,"

[44] In the Ugaritic root underlying *ddy* and *dd*, as postulated above, we have perhaps come upon the true etymology of Hebrew *zūd* (usually combined with Semitic *z-d*), " to boil over," also in anger or passion, " to be impudent, arrogant." Our two vocables, *mlḥmt* and *ddym*, have previously been rendered " combat " and " mandragores " (Virolleaud), " Fleischtopt " and " zwei Kruege " (Aistleitner), " war " and " passion " (Goetze).

most familiar to us in the pacific sense of the word. In the present context, however, the word must be seen to be employed in the less familiar, but very likely more primary, use of the vocable in the sense of " submission, surrender, capitulation "—a connotation especially alive and tenacious in Arabic, as witnessed by the meaning of *muslim* and *islām* in the time of Muhammad.

Our rendering of *l kbd* as " to the core of " is based on the assumption that this preposition, literally " to the liver of," is more comprehensive than *b qrb*, literally " in the bowels of." In the present context, it should perhaps be understood in the sense of " throughout the earth " and " throughout the land." [45]

Notwithstanding the lack of a word divider between the two vocables, we should not hesitate to read *arb dd*, and to see in *arb* a root closely related in meaning both with Hebrew *'ārab̲*, " to lurk, to lie in wait," and Arabic *'āraba*, " to strive to outwit, deceive or beguile " (3rd form), and " to overcome " (4th form), by superior wit or guile. As stated above, *dd* would seem to have a connotation very much like that of the Arabic verbal substantive *d̲aud*, that is, " the act of repelling or resisting." While " submission " and " resistance " form an antithesis, the locutions " pour out submission " and " overwhelm resistance," may readily be seen to represent a synonymous parallelism of the kind characteristic of

[45] Indeed the locution *l kbd arṣ* || *l kbd šdm* is elsewhere employed in a context that bespeaks intense searching (of Mot for his enemy Baal, and of Anat for the missing Baal) throughout the universe (*1AB* 2:16; *1*AB* 6:27). For *kbd* in the sense of " liver, entrails " (of vultures), see *1D* 130, etc.; in *5AB* B:25, we find *kbd* paralleled with *lb*, " heart " (of Anat); cf. Akkadian *libbu* and such Hebrew locutions as " the heart of the sea " (Exodus 15:8), " the heart of heaven " (Deuteronomy 4:11). Apparently, *šdm* (*šd-m?*) is here employed as a synonym of *arṣ*; cf. the use of *śād̲ê* in Ezekiel 25:6.

Ugaritic prosody. Apparently, it was the orthographic peculiarity whereby the word for "resistance" (*ḏōd*) and that for "love" (*dōd*) are written in the same way (*dd*), enhanced no doubt by the more common use of "peace" (*šlm*) in the refined sense of the word, which led to the suggestion that Baal's message to Anat was a proposal of love or even of marriage.[46]

This suggestion seems to have been further enhanced by the locution *šrḥq aṯt l pnn[h]* used by the narrator of *5AB* in a subsequent scene (D: 84) to describe an action undertaken by Baal at the moment he perceives that Anat, in response to his invitation, is now approaching his residence. The phrase has been translated "he sends away the women from his presence," as if in preparation of a love scene with Anat about to ensue.[47] In reality, the phrase must be understood in the sense "he makes his wives go (far) to meet her," that is, Baal honors the arrival of Anat by making his wives go a long distance to meet her and escort her to his presence —a procedure for receiving an honored female guest no doubt derived from the code of etiquette that prevailed in Ugaritic society.[48]

In support of this contention, as well as of the foregoing interpretation of the first part of Baal's message

[46] Goetze, the exponent of this interpretation, has even suggested a connection between the present unit of Baal's message to Anat (*Ba*) and the Christmas message (Luke 2: 4) and his article, above n. 1, is accordingly entitled "Peace on Earth."

[47] Gordon, *PL*, p. 55; also Herdner, *op. cit.*, p. 46 ("Il fait s'éloigner les femmes de sa présence").

[48] This would bear out the interpretation of *Aa* suggested above, cf. pp. 30 ff. For *rḥq* in the sense of "to go away, to withdraw," see *1K*, 3: 132, etc.; accordingly, *šrḥq* would denote causative action, "to make someone go away or withdraw"; cf. Hebrew *hirḥîq* used in the sense of *hirḥîq lā-leḵeṯ*, "he is gone (far) away" (Exodus 8: 24; contrast Genesis 44: 4; Joshua 8: 4). See the following note.

as a whole, reference may be made here to another encounter between Baal and Anat. It is described in a poem, designated by Virolleaud as *4AB*, that bears so strongly on the alliance-enmity motif that it may be cited and translated here in extenso. The encounter, together with an ensuing discourse of Baal, is recorded as follows (2:17-25):

1. bʿl (17) l pnnh ydd w yqm (18)
2. l pʿnh ykrʿ w yql (19)

3. w yśu gh w yṣḥ (20)
4. ḥwt axt w nar[t?] (21)

5. qrn dbatk btlt ʿnt (22)
6. qrn dbatk bʿl ymšḥ (23)
7. bʿl ymšḥh-m b ʿp (24)

8. nṭʿn b arṣ iby (25)
9. w b ʿpr qm axk

The above arrangement of the passage, while suggested by its wording, is open to question with regard to the difficulties offered by lines 4-6. If the arrangement be correct, *w nar* would almost certainly have been miswritten for *w nart*, by a kind of haplography, and we might discern here an N-stem formed either from a substantive *ar*, " light," or from a Qal " to be light." The stichos in question (*l.* 4) might thus be rendered:

May my sister live and shine,

which is highly improbable, however. Furthermore, the following stichos (*l.* 5) would then form a casus pendens, with the subject repeated and the verb supplied in the next stichos (*l.* 6), which is no less improbable. It would seem indeed that the difficulties have been caused by an erroneous addition, due to homoeoteleuton, of *dbatk*; that is, because of the occurrence of this word, after *qrn*, in the immediately following stichos. If so, the stichoi involved would read and scan thus:

4. ḥwt axt
5. w nar qrn btlt ʿnt

6. qrn dbatk bʿl ymšḥ
7. bʿl ymšḥh-m b ʿp,

and the whole passage may be translated as follows:

1. Baal runs to meet her, then he halts; [49]
2. (Now) he kneels at her feet and falls down.
3. Then he raises his voice and exclaims:
4. " May my sister live! [50]
5. And may the horn of the Virgin Anat sway! [51]
6. Thy scourging horn Baal will anoint,
7. Baal will anoint it with hardness: [52]

---

[49] So apparently also Virolleaud: " Baal au-devant d'elle court "; but in this case the Hebrew counterpart of *l pnn* is not *lip̄nê*, as suggested by Virolleaud, *Syria, 17*, 159, which would imply a movement " ahead of " or " before " Anat; rather, we deal here with the Ugaritic equivalent of Hebrew *liqraṯ* " toward, in the direction of," someone or something. It is thus tempting to see in *pnn* a verbal substantive (presumably a Piel) of a root identical with Hebrew **pnn* and related to Hebrew *pānâ*; literally, *l pnnh* would thus mean " to (the point of) facing her." We notice that in both passages the situation is the same—Baal had just perceived the approach of Anat—except that in *4AB* he himself runs to meet her, while in *5AB* he makes " his wives " do so. In passing, it may be remarked that the stichoi in *4AB* introducing the scene before us should be read and translated: *w yšu ʿnh w yʿn, w yʿn btlt ʿnt, nʿmt [ḥ]n axt, bʿl l pnnh ydd w yqm . . . ,* " When he lifts his eyes and looks, When he beholds the Virgin Anat, The [gra]ceful sweetness of his sister, Baal runs to meet her, then he halts," etc.

[50] On *ḥwt*, cf. Gordon, *UG*, 8.50 (hardly: mayest thou live, (o) my sister).

[51] Cf. *nʿr*, also *nʿr*, in Hebrew and Arabic (*LA*, 7, 39: *naʿara naʿiratun fi 'l-nāsi ḥājat hāʾijatun*).

[52] For *dbat*, cf. Arabic *dabaʾa* (*LA*, 1, 64: *dabaʾtuhu bi-'l- ʿaṣā dabʾan ḍarabtuhu*) and the *hap. leg. doḇʾeḵâ* (Deuteronomy 33:25, which cf.) rendered *hē ischus sou* in the LXX, and *tuqpāḵ* in Targum. I take *ʿp* (vocalize: *ʿappi*) to correspond to Arabic *ʿanf*, " severity, vehemence,

8. We shall thrust to the ground my enemies,
9. And to the dust the adversaries of thy brother." [53]

It is possible that, in line 7, we should read *ymšḥhm*, rather than *ymšḥh-m*, and understand *qrn* as "horns," that is, as a dual or a plural. We notice, at any rate, that, as similarly elsewhere in Semitic, "horn" is used here in the figurative sense of "potency, might, striking force," and we shall meet with another figurative use of *qrn* in the course of the present discussion. Again, in view of the connotation of *masaḥa* in Arabic, it is quite possible that Ugaritic employs the phrase of "annointing" one's horn in the meaning of "polishing" it, of making the "horn" bright and sharp.[54] The important thing at present is that, in the last couplet (*ll.* 8-9), Baal conveys to Anat the same aspiration which, in using different words, he conveys to her in the opening part of the message before us. For, by the phrasing and context of the two utterances, there can be no doubt that, except for the imperfect on the one hand and the imperatives on the other,

nṭ'n b arṣ iby
w b 'pr qm axk

is only another way of saying

qryy b arṣ mlḥmt
št b 'pr-m ddym,

harshness, rigorousness"; cf. Hebrew *'ānēp*, "to be wrathful," and see Micah 4:13 ("for thy horn I will make iron . . . and thou shalt crush many peoples"), 1 Kings 22:11, etc.

[53] It is obvious that *nṭ'n* should be combined with Arabic *ṭa'ana*, "to smite, pierce, wound, stab"; this may also be the meaning of *iṭ'nk* in *1*AB* 1:26. The writing *iby* makes it probable that both objects of *nṭ'n* are intended as plurals (*ēbīya, qāmī*). Remarkably enough, these two plurals may be found to form a parallelism in Hebrew poetry as well (2 Samuel 22:48; and elsewhere); see below, n. 65.

[54] Cf. the Septuagint on Habakkuk 3:4.

and that, accordingly, *qry* and *ṭ‘n*, *ib* and *mlḥm*, and *qm* and *ddy*, will have to be understood as representing pairs of close counterparts, if not indeed of outright synonyms.[55]

Bb. Haste Is Essential (*ll.* 17-20). Except for the last stichos (*l.* 20), the passage recurs in *6AB* as the concluding part of a message to Anat from El, to which we have referred above. Again in *6AB*, the entire passage, together with our *Bc*, forms the bulk of a message from El to Hayin. From the latter occurrence we learn that the initial word of the last stichos should read *tkṭh*, rather than *twṭh*, as read by Virolleaud, the signs for *w* and *k* being often all but indistinguishable on the Ugaritic tablets.

The first couplet of the passage is difficult, in both a syntactic and lexical respect, and the rendering suggested above may claim no more validity than that of a conjecture.[56] If it *is* a couplet, we would have here the only two stichoi within the entire discourse, or perhaps two of the only four stichoi (see *ll.* 23-24), which exhibit a two-stress meter. Possibly the phrase should be taken to represent a single, if overly long, stichos, intended to form a triplet with the two following stichoi (*ll.* 18-19): "Let thy compassion constrain thee (and) —or to—unite (?) thee with me."

It is safe to assume that in each of the three successive vocables with final *k*, the latter element represents the pronominal suffix of the second person singular, the

[55] In point of fact, synonymous usage of the first of the above pairs is listed by Arabic lexicographers; *Qamūs, 4,* 438: "*al-qarwu al-qaṣdu wal-tatabbu‘u . . . wal-ṭa‘nu,*" etc.; *Tāj al-‘Arūs, 10,* 292: "*yuqālu qarāhu 'iḏā ṭa‘anahu.*"

[56] The passage has been left untranslated by Albright, Gordon, Herdner ("le context . . . est obscur").

person being Anat, of course. But only the first mentioned vocable would seem to be a noun; as such, it should no doubt be identified with Arabic *ḥass or ḥiss,* "compassion, feeling (emotional), sense perception." The two other vocables may best be understood as perfect verbs with optative force. Thus taken, the phrase *ḥšk ʿṣk*; that is, *ḥaššuki ʿaṣāki,* would have a surprisingly close counterpart in such Syriac locutions as *ʿěṣāi ḥubbeh,* "his love constrained him" and, with a different verb, *ḥubbeh ʾāleṣ lan,* "his love constraineth us" (2 Corinthians 5:14). The object of Anat's constraint, which in Syriac would be described by a dependent *dě*-clause, would thus be stated here in the following asyndetic clauses. In other words, Baal here would suggest to his sister that her compassion or feeling for him should compel her to join him, or to join forces with him, to hasten to visit him, and to "stamp out" all "impudence," that is, presumably, to overcome any obstacles or handicaps that might hinder her journey to Mount Ṣapon.[57]

The rendering of *ʿbṣk,* that is *ʿabaṣaki,* as "let it (thy compassion) unite thee" is based on the assumption that we have here to do with an (assimilated?) form of the root * *ʿpṣ,* preserved in Arabic *ʿafaṣa,* "to tie, to bind, to fold, to bend," also "to coinhabit."[58] That *tlsmn* and *išdk* are to be combined, respectively, with Akkadian *lasāmu,* "to gallop, to run," and *išdu,* "sole, foot," has been noted by scholars before. Of the "vari-

[57] Virolleaud holds the entire series to consist of nouns ("ton verger, ton arbre, ton *ʿbṣ*"); Aistleitner takes the first vocable to be a verb ("nimm deinen Stab, deine Wegzehrung"). See Gesenius-Buhl, *s. v.* II *ḥwš* and *ʿṣh.*

[58] Cf. Virolleaud, *Anat* p. 34, "d'après une suggestion de M. Feghali"; for other instances of WS $p > b$ in Ugaritic, see "Incubation," p. 12, and n. 17.

ants " *twtḥ* and *tktḥ*, we should not hesitate to decide in favor of the latter, and recognize in it a Gt stem—*taktāḥ* or *taktāḥā*, depending on whether *išdk* represents a singular or a dual—of a verb identical with Arabic *kāḥa*, " to conquer, to overcome," and underlying the well known Hebrew *kōaḥ*, " power, might." [59]

Finally, I venture to suggest that *dm* be combined with Arabic *ḏimm*, *ḏamāmah*, and Hebrew *zimmâ*, " shame, impudence, blame, disgrace, lewdness," etc. As already indicated, we should understand the " impudence " in a subjective sense: any obstacle or interference that might threaten to prevent Anat from visiting Baal, her tread would stamp out as something shameful and disgraceful.[60]

Bc. Allusion to a Grand Plan (*ll.* 23-32). Merely by the length and the high rhetoric of this, the final section of the discourse, we would suspect that it was intended as the main and decisive part, the nervus rerum, of Baal's message to Anat. Yet the passage does not contain anything concrete and factual beyond Baal's statement to the effect that he wishes to confer with his sister—that is, confer with her orally and directly—the

[59] In all probability both *p'nk* and *išdk* are duals, while the difference between *tlsmn* and *tktḥ* is not that between *tqtln* (see Herdner, *RÉS*, 1938, p. 83) and *tqtl*, but rather that between *tqtl-n* and *tqtl*; in other words, we seem to deal here with another case of two optatives (*talsumā* and *taktāḥā*) of which the first is reinforced by the particle *na*; perhaps we should thus understand the series of jussives or cohortatives in *2D* 2:13 as well: *aṯb-n . . . w anx-n . . . w tnx* (rather than as a case of two energics followed by an indicative; cf. Gordon, *UG*, 8.8); see above, n. 37, and below, n. 78 and n. 93.

[60] I have always felt that, in *2AB* 3:20, 22, *tdmmt* should be understood as a verbal noun of *dmm* and vocalized, presumably, *tadmīmat*, " vilifying, corrupting, defiling, debauching," or the like; cf. Wright, *1*, 122 f.

implication being that this is why she should hasten to visit him. Rather than enlightening her here and now as to what it is he wishes to discuss with her, he merely tells her how crucial and important a thing it is. As a result, the passage abounds in mysterious hints and mystifying allusions about a plan or a scheme involving wood and stone, precious stone of an unheard-of and unprecedented nature, and connected, somehow, with Baal's own realm, the topos of " the God of Ṣapon."

The writer has dealt with the greater part of the passage (*ll.* 21-29) in a different connection.[61] At present it may therefore suffice to consider the details of the remainder of the passage. Admittedly, the interpretation suggested here, not only of the present unit but of the message as a whole, hinges on the stichos (*l.* 30)

at-m w ank ibǵyh,

specifically, on the meaning of *at.* Some scholars have seen in it the pronoun of the second person singular (*'atti*), the stichos having been rendered by Virolleaud " Vous et moi nous le haissons "; others have believed it to be an imperative (*'atī*): " Come and I shall show it." [62] But neither of these renderings yields a plausible

[61] " Negation," 238 f. One fails to see why *tant* (in *l.* 25), if it be a noun, would necessarily be repeated before *thmt* (*l.* 26), while no such repetition would be required if it be a verb (cf. Herdner, *op. cit.*, 83, n. 1). It should be needless to point out that a construct noun may be determined by more than one genitive, just as a verb may be qualified by more than one agent. In prose one might expect that the two genitives would be connected by a conjunction (*tant šmm . . . w thmt*), but even this is not " grammaticalement necessaire."

[62] Gordon, *PL*, p. 54, followed by Herdner, *RÉS*, 1942-45, p. 39 (" viens et moi je te le montrerai "); Albright, *op. cit.*, n. 11, takes *atm* to be an imperfect of *tmm*, " I shall make it (the thunderbolt) ready "; Aistleitner, *op. cit.*, p. 203, did suspect that *at* might be " ein dem Worte *rgm* paralleles Substantiv "; but he went no further than omitting *at* in his translation.

connection of the stichos with what precedes and what follows. In reality, the context of the passage—and indeed of the entire narrative—clearly suggests that we deal here with the last member of a series of appositives; namely, the series *hwt-rgm(‘ṣ)-tant-abn-rgm-at*, each member of the series intended to qualify the initial stichos: " I have (at heart) a thing I wish to tell thee," which forms the main clause of the whole passage. In this case, however, we should not fail to recognize in *at* the Ugaritic equivalent (*'ātu*) of Aramaic *'āṯā*, Hebrew *'ôṯ*, Arabic *'āyah*, and undoubtedly also of Akkadian *awātu* (*āwatu*?). In WS, the general sense of the word is " sign, mark," but its literary application may be seen to cover an exceedingly wide range of meaning: omen, proof, wonder, miracle, warning, symbol, evidence, standard, figure, example, memorial, etc. Almost any of these meanings would fit as a rendering of *at*. But I venture to submit that " monument " comes nearest to what the Ugaritic narrator had in mind. In Akkadian, *awātu* is used in the sense of Ugaritic *rgm* and Hebrew *dāḇār*, that is, in the sense of " word, thing, affair, concern," and this agrees with the use of Arabic *'āyah* for spoken or written " utterance, communication, message," of a person or, in the Koran, of Allah; also with the use of the vocable in Aramaic for " sound, letter," of the alphabet. Perhaps, then, *rgm*, *hwt*, *at*, were felt to be synonyms or quasi-synonyms by the Ugaritic poets.

It is barely possible that *w ank ibġyh* represents a copulative-parenthetical clause: " and I do desire it " or " and I much desire it." It would seem safe, however, to analyze the stichos, at least superficially, as a relative clause annexed, by means of *w*, to the substantive *at-m* (which latter would thus be understood as a *ṣifah* rather than a *ṣilah*). In other words, we would be faced here, and apparently also in two other stichoi of the present section (*ll.* 21-22), with the Ugaritic peculiarity concerning the positional freedom of *w*, which we have considered above (*l.* 6). If so, our stichos—and, *mutatis mutandis*, the two other stichoi—will have to be recognized as standing in lieu of *w at-m ank ibġyh*, "And (it concerns) a monument I much desire." In either case, we may assume, the series of adverbial qualifications in what immediately follows (*ll.* 31-33) is intended to define the locale of *at-m*, and indirectly of the "thing" that Baal is to discuss with Anat during her forthcoming visit, rather than the locale of *ibġyh*.

The series is as significant in its context as it is impressive in its eloquence and emphasis. It is as if Baal had been made by the poet to leave nothing unsaid in order to impress Anat with the all-decisive importance of, and with his own claim to, the "Mount" that was to serve as the locale of the plan he had at heart and was so eager to convey to her. We notice, in particular, that in contrast to a series we have considered above (*ll.* 2-5), the preposition here (*b*) is repeated no fewer than five times, that is, before each member of the series—presumably for additional emphasis. We also notice that the pronominal suffix of *ġry*, "the mountain of mine," is significantly qualified, appositionally, by *il ṣpn*, "God of Ṣapon." In *ṣpn*, literally "Height," *qdš*, "Holiness," *n'm*, "Delight," we apparently have to do with quasi proper names or hypostases comparable to *haq-qōḏeš*, as a designation of the sanctuary of the Temple of Jerusalem, also of the Tabernacle. It is because of these designations that one is led to see in *tliyt* another hypostatized appellative, presumably "Endeavor" or "Effort," and thus to combine it with

Hebrew *tĕlā'â* and Aramaic *lĕ'ūṯā*, "burden, labor, effort, care." [63]

The Message as a Whole. Specifically as regards the last two units of the message, *Bb* and *Bc*, it is of methodological importance to recall once again that, according to *6AB*, these units formed the main body of a message, not from Baal to Anat, but rather from El to Hayin. It is the supreme god El who in *6AB* orders an envoy, apparently none other than his daughter Anat, to go to Egypt, the domain of Hayin, in order to apprise the great master-builder, first, that he should hasten to visit him and, second, that he, El, desires to confer with him concerning a very grave and confidential matter. The notion, therefore, that the same message when found in *5AB* has to do with an invitation to a romantic tête-à-tête collapses before our eyes once again. Instead, we find ourselves confronted with the question of how to understand a scene assigned, in different epical poems, to different sets of gods, although the personal characters of the gods concerned—El, Baal, Anat, Hayin—appear to remain constant throughout the epic. To put it differently: what is that weighty and mysterious "thing" which in one poem (*5AB*) Baal wishes to say to Anat and in another poem (*6AB*) El is eager to con-

[63] We recall that, in utterances of YHWH, Mt. Zion is frequently referred to as *har qoḏšî* ("my Mount Holiness"?), and occasionally also as *naḥlāṯî*, "my inheritance" (Jeremiah 12:7; 16:18); cf. *JBL*, *55* (1936), 21 ff. As a designation of Mt. Ṣapon *ǵr tliyt* occurs also in *4AB* (3:29, 32), where it is paralleled with *ǵr mslmt*; it is tempting to see in the latter designation still another hypostatized epithet of Ṣapon, possibly in the sense of "Stairway, Ladder"; cf. the "ladder" (*sullām*) leading from earth to heaven—or better, from the earthly to the heavenly sanctuary—in Jacob's dream, which has been combined by modern critics with the temple-tower of Bablyonia and the eschatological "ladder" of Egypt and Persia; see the commentaries on Genesis 28:10-12 (Gunkel, Skinner); cf. *slmt* in Phoenician (*CIS*, 1, 88.4, 5).

vey to Hayin? And how may we understand that the master-builder not only follows El's summons but, in still another poem (*2AB*), accepts a commission from Baal to bring his desire for a house to final realization, while, in yet another poem (*3AB*), he helps Baal destroy an enemy who, with the support of El, threatens to frustrate that desire?

Thus, as regards any reliable interpretation of the message, it is obvious that its decisive test lies in the extent to which it is borne out not only by the subsequent progress of the narrative within our tablet, but by related narratives in different tablets. That is to say, only such an interpretation may claim philological validity as renders the message a consistent and integrated part of the ensuing action and of the various ramifications appertaining to it. In the perusal of that action as evidenced in the text of *5AB*, we find (*a*) that, after Baal's envoy has delivered the message to her, Anat at once proceeds to visit her brother; (*b*) that during that visit she is commissioned by him to go to El and lay before him the "complaint" about his lack of a house; (*c*) that she not only accepts the commission but is confident of achieving its purpose, if necessary, by the use of force; (*d*) that she then goes before El and actually threatens him with violence should he refuse to accede to Baal's request; and (*e*) that after her negotiations with El—the conclusion of which is missing in the tablet—have been completed, Baal dispatches his envoy to the master-builder Hayin.

At this point, it is true, the text of *5AB* breaks off. But in following the action from this point on as it is described in *2AB*, we further learn (*f*) that, upon Hayin's arrival, Baal orders him to erect a palace *b mrym ṣpn*, "on the Height of Ṣapon"; (*g*) that, in executing Baal's order, Hayin builds a house of gold and silver, with the precious cedars of Lebanon providing wood to serve as smelting fuel; and (*h*) that the first thing Baal does after the house is built and the completion duly feasted is to inform his adversary Mot of the success of the undertaking: " Of silver I have (now) built my house, of gold I have wrought my palace."

We need only bring these main points of the drama to bear on Baal's message to become at once aware that it represents the starting point of the building epic; that is, at least, the starting point of the epic *apud 5AB*: an invitation to Anat to join forces with Baal and to ally herself with his plan of building a house of an extraordinary kind. Conversely, once we realize that the " thing " he intended to convey to her during her visit was none other than his building scheme, we find the suspense so artfully created by the message, with all its mystifying hints and allusions, is gradually and cunningly dissolved as we follow the narrative from scene to scene: the allusion to wood and stone; the reference to unheard-of " stone of splendor," unheard-of and unprecedented no doubt because of the great profusion in which it is to be made available; the hint of a " monument " at the topos of the " God of Ṣapon."

Indeed, we shall see presently that the features in Baal's message that are particularly mystifying—his request of Anat to purge the " warriors " and " repellers," his implied reluctance to entrust knowledge of his plan even to his envoy, his explicit reference to the " secret " of stone, the great stress he puts on " my mountain " and " my inheritance "—are admirably clarified in the very first scene that follows his charge to the envoy: the scene ensuing upon the envoy's arrival at the presence of Anat. Baal's message, it then becomes apparent, is an invitation to Anat to join forces with him against his enemies—an invitation to conspiracy no less than alliance.

Nor is it now in the least difficult to understand how in a different Ugaritic narrative—or, as we should no doubt say, according to a different Ugaritic tradition—it is El who cherishes the ambitious desire of building for himself an extraordinary and unheard-of kind of "monument," but that, unlike Baal, he dispatches the crucial message directly to Hayin: as the supreme god, El naturally stands in no need of having his desire approved by any other god.

III. ENEMIES AND RIVALS

In the main, the scene between Anat and Baal's envoy (D:32-80) consists of three direct discourses. First (*ll.* 32-48), the goddess addresses Gepen-and-Ugar; second (*ll.* 49-64), the latter delivers to her Baal's message; last (*ll.* 65-75), Anat replies to the message, and adds (*ll.* 76-80) a statement of her own. When all the details have been clarified to a greater extent than they now are, the scene will warrant a study of its own. The general trend, however, is sufficiently clear to permit an analysis of the scene as a whole.

Anxiety and Counsel (*ll.* 32-48). In a descriptive preamble to the scene (*ll.* 29-32), the narrator relates how, upon perceiving the arrival of Baal's envoy, Anat is seized with great anxiety and trepidation, her feet tremble, her loins quake, etc. An identical description, it has been noted, may be found in *2AB* (2:11-20) applied to Athirat; but the identity in wording, it goes without saying, need not necessarily indicate a single narrator. For in both instances the description appears to be employed for the purpose of introducing parallel scenes: request for aid and assistance in behalf of Baal, the prospective ministrant being Athirat in *2AB*, and Anat in the text before us. In other words, we merely have here another instance of the stylistic phenomenon which we have repeatedly noticed above; namely, the use of literary clichés to describe a standard situation, the situation before us being that of a deity being seized with sudden anguish.[64]

[64] As far as one can see, Cassuto (*BJPES*, *10*, 2-3, 1943, 52 ff.) was the first to interpret the passage properly and to recognize the basic nature

But whence the anguish and anxiety? Why should Anat, the fierce and fearless, tremble and quake at the mere sight of a messenger from her favorite brother? The explanation is supplied by the goddess herself. Having sufficiently recovered to welcome the envoy with the customary greeting formula " How has Gepen-and-Ugar come! " Anat exclaims

mn ib ypʿ l bʿl
ṣrt l rkb ʿrpt

What enemies have risen unto Baal?
What rivals, unto the Rider of Clouds? [65]

---

of the parallelism; but I have never been able to accept his suggestion that the goddesses' apprehension is to be understood as caused solely by the unexpected arrival of visitors—especially, since the visitors are, in *5AB*, messengers from the goddess' favorite brother and, in *2AB*, her son and daughter. Moreover, the suggestion is rendered untenable by the complacent joy of El at the unexpected visit of his spouse (*2AB* 4-5 : 27 ff.), while Daniel's reaction to the good tidings that he was to beget a son (*2D* 2 : 10 ff.; cf. " Incubation," pp. 22 f.) is " analogous " only if we recognize, as we should, that the goddesses are dismayed because they surmise that Baal is threatened by enemies and in need of their help (against Ginsberg, *BASOR*, *98*, 16, n. 20). The lengthy passage describing the visit of Baal and Anat with Athirat (*2AB* 2 : 12 to 4-5 : 19) is badly damaged; but there can be no doubt that the purpose of their visit was to " emplore " and " entreat " (3 : 28, *tmgnn* . . . *tǵẓyn*) their mother to ally herself with Baal and, in particular, to intercede in his behalf with El; see below, n. 73.

[65] It should be obvious that *mn* here is an interrogative pronoun, as seen by Aistleitner (" Welcher Feind "), and not a " simple form " of the general pronoun *mnm* (against *UG*, 5. 42); nor need this be forestalled by the use in Ugaritic of *my*, " who? " (*UG*, 5. 44); the two interrogative pronouns may very well have been employed, respectively, in substantival (" who? ") and adjectival (" which? ") sense; cf. Arabic *man* and *aiyun*. Although a grammatical singular, *ib* should no doubt be understood as a collective and, accordingly, *ṣrt* as a plural (*ṣarrāt*; above, p. 40); cf. *iby* in the passage we have cited from *4AB*, and the frequent collective connotation of *'ôyēḇ* in the Old Testament. Note that, like the Hebrew equivalents of *ib* and *qm* (above n. 53), so also those of *ib* and *ṣrt* may be found combined, often by parallelism, in biblical writings (Isaiah 1 : 24; Nahum 1 : 2, etc.). In *ypʿ* (probably a perfect: *yapaʿa*)

And without waiting for an answer, Anat breaks forth into a passionate flow of boastful exclamations recounting how she did or, possibly, how she will—the verbs she employs being mostly in the perfect tense [66]—" crush," " destroy," " seize," " cram down," a variety of gods, to wind up with the astonishing stichos in the imperfect tense

imtxṣ w itrš xrṣ

(Thus) I will batter on and inherit gold!

In a somewhat calmer and, apparently, more reflective mood, the goddess now turns to the envoy to address him as follows:

1. ṭrd bʿl (45) b mrym ṣpn
2. mšṣṣ w ʿṣr (46) udnh
3. gršh l ksi mlkh (47)

4. l nxt l kḥṯ drkth (48)
5. mnm ib ypʿ l bʿl
6. ṣrt 1 rkb ʿrpt

This passage appears to have puzzled scholars, and, as far as one can see, no plausible rendering has hitherto been advanced. It would therefore seem advisable to consider the passage in detail before venturing to suggest a new translation.

Seen superficially, the passage might be understood as arranged in three couplets and has actually been so understood. Upon closer scrutiny, one cannot help dis-

we have clearly come upon the root underlying Hebrew *hôp̄iaʿ*, " to appear, to arrive," also causative (awkwardly rendered in dictionaries " to shine, to glitter," Bauer-Leander, p. 383: " Licht verbreiten "), which in rabbinical Hebrew may be found used with hostile connotation; cf. Jastrow, *s. v. yāp̄aʿ*.

[66] Cf. Herdner, *op. cit.*, p. 43, n. 3.

cerning here two triplets, as suggested by the above division, with the interstrophical parallelism being more pronounced than the interlinear one. But what seems to have encumbered a satisfactory interpretation of the passage is not so much the question of arrangement as rather a series of syntactic and lexical misapprehensions, enhanced, apparently, by the use of the pronominal suffix "his" (*h*) to refer to different persons, and by the same particle (*l*) employed for different functions.

The difficulties begin with the initial phrase *ṭrd bʿl* and the parallel *grš̌h*, rendered by Virolleaud, and similarly by others, "Fonce, ô Baal . . . chasse-le," which is plainly untenable, since Baal is not present.[67] In reality, there can be little doubt that we have here to do, not with imperatives, but with optative perfects: "Let Baal banish" (*ṭarada*), "Let him expel him" (*garrašahu*).[68] The direct object of both verbs, to which the suffix of *gršh* refers, is represented by two adjectival nouns: (*a*) *mšṣṣ*, an intensive participle (*maśaṣṣiṣ*), the meaning of which may easily be inferred from Arabic *šaṣṣa*, "to hinder, to hold back, to be hard, troublesome"; and (*b*) *ʿṣr udnh*, another participle (*ʿāṣir*) qualified by an accusative or genitive (*ʾudnahu* or *ʾudnihu*),[69] yielding a

[67] For other renderings, cf. Aistleitner ("die Baal vertreiben wollen . . . die ihn vertreiben wollen"); Herdner ("Baʿal a-t-il été chassé . . . l'a-t-on chassé?"); Gordon, *UG*, 3.16 (*ṭrd*, "drive out!").

[68] The use of the perfect with optative force is much more frequent in Ugaritic texts than has been generally realized. As in the instance before us, failure to recognize optative connotation of a given perfect, or a series of perfects, has often led to unnecessary "exegesis" as well as grammatical misstatements.

[69] It is impossible to determine with certainty whether Ugaritic nouns were inflected as to case endings when followed by possessive suffixes, in agreement with Arabic and Ethiopic; but to judge by the evidence from Akkadian (Ungnad, *Babylonisch-Assyrische Grammatik*, 25.*a*), one would be inclined to assume that Ugaritic did employ case endings before suffixes, though not in the construct in general. I have always held that

phrase reminiscent of the biblical " who stoppeth his ear," which phrase would appear to be employed in Ugaritic in the sense of " disobedient, insurgent," or the like. The root *'ṣr* may be found elsewhere in Semitic to denote the act of " withholding, arresting," while " withholding one's ear " has its counterpart in locutions that signify the lending of one's ear, found in Hebrew and, it seems, in Ugaritic itself.[70]

Because of the preceding *l ksi* and the following *l kḥṯ*, also no doubt because the passage involved has been held to form a couplet, the phrase *l nxt* is translated by Virolleaud " du repos," as if we had here a substantive derived from *n-x*, which root is actually employed in Ugaritic, and elsewhere, in the sense of " to rest, to repose." What is more, in the Ugaritic Keret narrative we come upon a passage which at first sight seems to form a close parallel with the passage before us (*ll.* 3-4), and in which *nxt* could hardly mean anything but " rest, repose," or the like; while still another occurrence of the vocable, in *2AB* (1:34), may be found in close proximity to *kḥṯ*, " throne, seat." At the same time, however, " du repos " is so entirely out of keeping with the present context that Virolleaud has felt obliged to suspect *l nxt* to be a gloss here.[71]

this should be assumed for WS in general (cf. Bauer-Leander, *Hist. Gr.*, pp. 254, 523; *Gr. d. Bibl.-Aram.*, p. 76). It goes without saying that, at any rate, a cluster such as *udnhu* or *malkna* (see below, n. 91) is hardly conceivable.

[70] On *šṣṣ*, see *LA*, 8, 314 (". . . *al šaṣā'iṣ al-šadā'id* . . . *wašaṣṣahu 'an al-šai'i wa-'ašaṣṣahu mana'ahu* ") and Lane, *s. v.* For locutions of the kind before us, cf. Proverbs 21:13, " who stoppeth (*'ôṭēm*) his ear "; Isaiah 33:15, " stoppeth his ear . . . and shutteth (*'ôṣēm*) his eyes "; specifically, on *'āṣar*, cf. Genesis 20:18; Job 4:2, Numbers 17:13, etc.; see also " Negation," n. 25.

[71] *Anat*, p. 58: " l *nḫt* — ' pour le repos ' est donc, sinon une glose, du moins une formule explicative," etc. Presumably because of this difficulty,

It is therefore not too venturesome to propose that we are faced here with the well-known circumstance, even more frequent in Ugaritic than generally in Semitic texts, of unrelated vocables being written in exactly the same way, while the vocables in question may or may not be homonyms. One need only think of instances like Hebrew *naḥaṯ*, " descent, coming down " and " rest, ease," or Hebrew *šeḇeṯ*, " dwelling, sitting " and " cessation," to realize that our *nxt* need not be an abstract of *n-x*, as in the Keret passage, nor a participle of *n-x* (*nāxat*), as in the *2AB* occurrence, but rather a perfect verb identical with Arabic *naxata*, " to pull off, to snatch away, to tear off." [72] In this case, we would have before us another optative, with Baal as its agent, corresponding in syntax and meaning with *ṭrd* and *gršh*, so that the preceding *l* would represent the precative particle *lu* rather than the preposition *li*. Indeed, to judge by an Aramaic locution like *honḥaṯ min kursē malḵūṯeh* (Daniel 5 : 20)—which sounds almost like a paraphrase of our *nxt l kḥṯ drkth*—one might suspect that *nxt*, in the meaning just mentioned, had been extant in NWS before it coalesced with *nḥt*. The important thing is that *mnm ib*, " whatever enemy " may now be recognized as the direct object of *nxt*, and need no longer be confused, as it has been, with the interrogative *mn ib*, " what

l nxt, in the passage before us, has been rendered " vom Sitze " (Aistleitner *op. cit.*) and, in Keret (unnecessarily!), " upon his dais " (Ginsberg, *2K* 6 : 24); but this rendering presupposes a semantic development not supported in the text, nor does it entirely clarify the context.

[72] See Lane, *s. v.*, and *LA*, *2*, 404 (*wal-naxtu wal-natfu wāḥidun*). It can be demonstrated conclusively, I believe, that in *2AB*, *nxt* must be taken to be a feminine participle qualifying *kḥt il*, in the sense of " resting "; such a demonstration, however, would require a critical analysis of the contextual unit in which the phrase occurs; I intend to deal with the difficult passage (*ll.* 31-44) upon another occasion.

enemy?" or "what enemies?" at the beginning of Anat's discourse. The whole passage then may be rendered as follows:

1. Let Baal banish from the Height of Ṣapon
2. (Anyone) who makes trouble and withholds his obedience;
3. Let him expel him from the seat of his kingdom.
4. Yea, let him pluck out from the throne of his reign
5. Whatever enemies have risen unto Baal,
6. (Whatever) rivals, unto the Rider of Clouds.

In effect, Anat here volunteers her counsel as to how Baal should secure his realm against dangers from within. Having first indicated her readiness to meet any assault that might threaten him from the gods at large, and thus put herself in the sole possession of gold—the obvious implication being that the gold inherited from the subdued enemy would be made to serve Baal's interests—she now tells her brother, through the medium of his envoy, that he must suppress in his own topos any and all trends of revolt and insurgence, in order to make his reign on the height of Ṣapon supreme and absolute.

Ultimately, one cannot fail to realize, we deal here with a skillful literary device aimed to heighten the tension of the dramatic narrative. The poet describes Anat's anxiety at the mere appearance of the messenger, because he makes her surmise the nature of message: Baal is threatened by rivals and enemies. But he makes her foresee only part of Baal's errand. When, presently, the message is delivered to her, she learns that her anxiety was indeed well-founded: Baal did need her help to purge the warriors and repellers, he was really concerned about a "secret of stone," and "stone of splendor," and he did appeal to his right and claim to the Height of Ṣapon, the mount of his inheritance. But she also learns that there was much more to her brother's message which she failed to guess: something of so vital an import that Baal would not entrust it even to his envoy, something that she would be told only in the privacy of a personal encounter with her brother.

The dramatic device, however, we must further realize, would be lost and pointless unless the narrator could count on the full response and understanding of his listeners. He cannot but have been certain that they would follow and appreciate Anat's reaction to the arrival of Gepen-and-Ugar, because such would have been their own reaction. The same must, of course, be said to apply to the identical device in the description in *2AB* of Athirat's dismay and misgivings, to which we have referred. In short, we are all but forced to infer that, in both instances, the narrator made use of a popular belief held in Ugaritic folklore: a belief that Baal was forever threatened by rivals and adversaries, that the main issue involved was his supremacy over the Height of Ṣapon, and that the outcome of the struggle depended on the control and possession of what Baal guardedly described as "the stone of splendor," but which was bluntly and unwittingly referred to as "gold" in the excited premonition of Anat.[73]

[73] Although the corresponding scene in *2AB* is badly damaged, it can be seen to exhibit the same trend of thought as the scene between Anat and Gepen-and-Ugar. Like Anat here, so Athirat in *2AB* is dismayed at the arrival of Baal and Anat because she suspects that Baal is threatened by his enemies. To judge by what is discernible on Virolleaud's photo (Pl. XXX, cf. Pl. XXV), the first words uttered by the goddess, following the greeting formula, would seem to have been (*ll.* 24-26): *mxṣ y*[*m*(*t?*)]*xṣ bny, h*[*lm y*(*t?*)*lm ṣ*]*brt aryy,* "Does a smiter s[mi]te my children? [Does] a ba[tterer batter the f]lock of my kin?" Again, like Anat in the scene before us, so Athirat is made to betray her awareness of the great importance of gold for the cause of Baal. She recovers from her

Delivery of the Message (*ll.* 49-64). It is remarkable that, when the goddess had finished, Baal's envoy takes notice of her rhetorical outburst with but a single couplet—and this a couplet borrowed from her own discourse:

l ib ypʿ l bʿl
ṣrt l rkb ʿrpt,

before embarking at once upon the main business of his errand; namely, the verbatim delivery of his master's message, beginning with "Thus spoke Aliyan Baal." It is further noteworthy that not a word is said to the effect that he also attended to the part of his errand that called for "a gem" to be put on Anat's breast. Perhaps we should understand that the omission of a corresponding reference was deliberate, the narrator being mindful not to interrupt the flow of the close-knit dialogue.

It has been suggested by scholars that the initial element of the couplet just cited might represent the common Semitic adverb of negation *lā*, so that it would have to be rendered "No enemy," etc.[74] Except for the unmistakable implications of the context, this suggestion would deserve serious consideration, since we know now—and, if further demonstration be needed, such a demonstration is provided, as we shall see, by

dismay only when realizing that her "children" had brought precious metals with them (presumably this was referred to at the, now missing, beginning of column 3 of *2AB*). I venture to submit that *ll.* 26 ff. be restored thus: [*ẓl*] *ksp aṯrt k tʿn, ẓl ksp w n*[*r*] *xrṣ, śmx rbt atrt ym*, "(Yet) when Athirat beheld [the shadow] of silver, the shadow of silver and the gl[itter] of gold, then did Lady Athirat of the Sea rejoice"; presumably, "shadow" is here used in the sense of "glimmer, shimmer," or the like; perhaps this is also the case of *ṣēl hak-kesep̄*, in Ecclesiastes 7:12, "For the glimmer of Wisdom is like the glimmer of silver."

[74] So first, it seems, Aistleitner, *op. cit.*: "Kein (?) Feind"; hesitatingly, also Herdner, *op. cit.*, p. 44.

Baal's message as delivered by the envoy—that the negative particle *lā* is actually employed in Ugaritic for sentence negation, and there is no reason why it should not have been used for word negation as well. As it is, however, the present scene as a whole and each of its parts require that the couplet be understood as a direct, and indeed emphatic, confirmation of Anat's misgivings on the part of Gepen-and-Ugar:

> Forsooth, enemies have risen unto Baal,
> Rivals, unto the Rider of Clouds!

We would thus be led to posit that the asseverative particle *la* is used in Ugaritic as a prefix of nouns no less than of verbs, as it is commonly so used in Arabic.[75]

As compared with the text of the message when it was first uttered by Baal, which we have reproduced above (p. 23 f.), its repetition by the envoy exhibits a number of scribal variants of the kind that seem to be unavoidable in Ugaritic parallel passages of any length. One of these variants involves a difference in the succession of certain stichoi. The difference may best be illustrated if we retain the numbers of the corresponding stichoi as evidenced in the first occurrence of the message but follow their order in the present occurrence:

23. rgm ʿṣ
24. w lxšt (59) abn

28. rgm l tdʿ nšm

---

[75] Another clear instance of the asseverative particle *l* prefixed to a noun may be seen in the phrase *uġr l rḥq il-m*, which I take to mean "*uġr* is furthest away from the god" (*5AB* D:78; cf. *6AB* 3:19). On the use of *la* in Arabic, see Wright *1*, 282 f.; as first observed by Paul Haupt, the particle may be seen to have been employed in Hebrew as well (Brockelmann, *Grundriss*, *2*, 110); here, on the contrary, it appears to have been prefixed to nouns only. See below, n. 78.

29. w l tbn (60) hmlt arṣ
25. tant šmm ‘m arṣ (61)
26. thmt ‘mn kbkbm

27. abn brq (62) dl td‘ šmm
30. at-m w ank (63) ibġyh
31. b tk ġry il ṣpn . . .

23. (It's) a thing about wood,
24. And a secret about stone:
28. A thing that men have not known,
29. And the multitudes of the earth have not perceived.
25. (It's) the contention of the heavens with the earth,
26. Of the deep with the stars.
27. (It's) stone of splendor, which the heavens have not known;
30. (It concerns) a monument that I do desire,
31. Amid the mountain of mine, God of Ṣapon . . .

It stands to reason that a confusion in the order of the stichoi such as the one before us may best be understood as effected by the circumstance that the text makes sense in either of the two successions.[76] One might even feel inclined to see in the passage just quoted the original succession of stichoi, since the balance here seems more plausible than it is in the first occurrence. This, however, is the case only when the particle *l* in the second couplet (*ll.* 28-29) is properly understood as *lā*, the adverb of negation. To mistake it for the precative particle, as it has been mistaken, is to be faced with the incoherence of the " secret of stone " being qualified as " a thing that men may know." [77]

Invitation Accepted (*ll.* 65-75a). The delivery of Baal's message, by his envoy, is followed immediately

[76] *Cf.* " Incubation," p. 14*b*, last paragraph.

[77] Gordon, *PL*, p. 54; Albright, *op. cit.*: " that men may know the command."

by a lengthy reply of Anat (*ll.* 65-80). Only part of this reply, we have seen, is in direct response to the message, while the rest of Anat's statement (*ll.* 76b-80) introduces a new theme, an afterthought, as it were. This is clearly indicated by the narrator who makes the goddess preface her remarks with the formula,

ap mṯn rgm-m argm-n

Moreover, another thing let me say.[78]

Accordingly, Anat's sole articulate reaction to the substance of the message just delivered to her may be found in the passage preceding the above formula:

1. w tʿn btlt ʿnt
2. ṯṯb (66) [ymmt?] limm
3. [hlm?] aqry (67) b arṣ mlḥmt
4. ašt b ʿpr-m (68) ddym
5. ask šlm l kbd arṣ (69)
6. arb dd l kbd šdm

[78] It is tempting to see here still another instance of an optative imperfect reinforced by *na* (cf. above n. 59, also n. 37), which would yield a much smoother context than would an energicus. Moreover, it would furnish us with the Ugaritic counterpart of a corresponding locution frequent in Hebrew: a speaker politely inviting attention to what he has to say by using a cohortative of a verbum dicendi, or a jussive, with *na*—according to whether he refers to himself in the first person (2 Samuel 14:15, "let me speak"; 1 Kings 1:2, "let me advise thee"; 2 Kings 7:12, "let me tell you"; Isaiah 5:1, 5, "let me sing . . . let me inform you"; etc.) or in the third person (Genesis 44:18, "let thy servant speak," 1 Samuel 25:24, "let thy handmaid speak," etc.). The additional "thing" which Anat here conveys to Baal's envoy is also conveyed, in *6AB*, to El's envoy by Hayin. While lexically difficult, the passage may be seen to describe the exceedingly long distance between the residence of Anat and that of Baal (*5AB*) and between the residence of Hayin and that of El (*6AB*); it is obvious that *6AB* 3:18b f. should be restored, against Virolleaud, to read [*kptr*] *l rḥq ilm, ḥkpt l rḥq ilnym*; cf. above, n. 75. Since El's envoy to Hayin must be seen to be Anat, the phrase *atm bštm*, occurring in both passages, cannot be used (as it is by Ginsberg, *BASOR*, 95, 27) in support of the thesis that *gpn w ugr* represents names of two messengers of Baal; see above, n. 28.

7. yšt (70) [aliyn] bʿl mdlh
8. ybʿr (71) [rkb ʿrp]t [q]rnh

9. aqry (72) [ank?] b arṣ mlḥmt (73)
10. ašt b ʿpr-m ddym

11. ask (74) šlm l kbd arṣ
12. arb dd (75) l kbd šdm

Except for a single couplet, the passage appears to be both familiar and repetitious. Anat begins, so it would seem, with a declaration of her readiness to purge the "warriors" and "repellers" (*ll.* 3-6), thereby borrowing Baal's formulation in every detail, substituting only first person imperfects for his imperatives: *aqry* for *qryy, ašt* for *št, ask* for *sk.* She then (*ll.* 7-8) offers a couplet of her own wording. Finally (*ll.* 9-12), she expresses anew her acceptance of Baal's bidding by repeating the declaration with which she had begun. Yet, in itself awkward, this understanding of the passage is rendered dubious by two lacunae, one at the beginning of the first unit (*l.* 3) and another following the *aqry* of the last unit (*l.* 9).

Obviously, a critical interpretation of the passage depends on the nature of these lacunae and, above all, on the couplet of Anat's own making. Although badly mutilated on the tablet, and left open by Virolleaud, the couplet may be reliably restored in every particular. We notice at a glance that, between *yšt* and *bʿl,* the element effaced must have been *aliyn;* similarly, that, between *ybʿr* and *t,* there can only have stood *rkb ʿrp.* Again, by the testimony of the scene from *4AB* which we have cited above (p. 43), we realize that *rnh* should be restored to read *qrnh.* The question is thus reduced to the meaning of *mdl* and the application of *qrn.* It will be seen, however, that if *ybʿr* may be combined with

Hebrew *bāʿar*, we would obtain here a locution to the effect that Baal will " ignite "—or " illuminate "—" his horn," a counterpart to his " anointing " or " polishing, brightening " of Anat's horn in *4AB*. We recall, too, that " horn " may also be used figuratively for " dominion, rule," both in Hebrew and Aramaic, as best illustrated by the application of the vocable in the Book of Daniel (7 : 24; 8 : 21, etc.). It is thus tempting to see in the parallel *mdl* a corresponding meaning by combining it with Arabic *'idālah, dawlah,* " victory, predominance, sovereignty." [79]

Whether or not this is the precise meaning of *mdl*, and the actual application of *qrn* intended by the narrator, the general sense of the couplet is clearly to the effect that Baal will be successful and his aspirations will prevail. Accordingly, it is all but unavoidable to see in the couplet, not an independent sentence, but rather an apodosis of the sentence beginning with [. . .] *aqry*, and to assume that the missing element was a subordinating particle, such as *hlm*, " when," *ʿd*, " until," *hm*, " if," *axr*, " after," or some other temporal or causal conjunction.[80] In this case, however, only the last part of Anat's reply (*ll*. 9-12) would be an independent sentence and only here would she declare her unqualified

[79] For Ugaritic *bʿr*, see also *2AB* 4-5 : 16, *šbʿr* . . . *k kbkb*, "(and) brightens . . . like a star"; perhaps also *1K* 2 : 101: *ybʿr l ṯn aṯth*, if this may be taken to mean " he renders fervent his wife for (the benefit of) another"; cf. Ugaritic *ḥmḥm*, Hebrew *yḥm* (see *LK*, p. 16). In the sense suggested above, *mdl* would be a noun like *mqm* (from *q-m*), *mṣd* (from *ṣ-d*), and should be listed as " *mdl* III " (cf. *UG*, Glossary, p. 102), while " *mdl* II " should perhaps be seen as a derivative of *dly/w*, whence Akkadian *dalū*, Hebrew *dĕlî*, " pail," used in Aramaic also for the zodiacal " Aquarius."

[80] In favor of *hlm* is the use of this particle as one of subordination elsewhere in *5AB* (D : 29): " when (or as soon as) Anat sees the gods . . ."

readiness to act according to Baal's bidding, while the missing word that followed *aqry* would fittingly have been designed to give her promise added emphasis: *ank*, " I, myself " or " I indeed," possibly *bkm*, " thus, and so," or the like. Anat's response to her brother's invitation would therefore read as follows:

1. And there answered the Virgin Anat,
2. There replied the [Yamamat] of the People:
3. " [When] I strike the warriors to the ground,
4. Put to the dust the repellers,
5. Pour out submission to the core of the earth,
6. Overcome resistance to the core of the land,
7. Then will [Aliyan] Baal establish his sovereignty,
8. Then will [the Rider of Cloud]s ignite his [h]orn!
9. I [indeed] will strike the warriors to the ground,
10. I will put to the dust the repellers,
11. Will pour out submission to the core of the earth,
12. Overcome resistance to the core of the land!

It is significant that Anat does not reply at all to the main point of Baal's message: to the " thing " about " wood " and " stone," about " stone of splendor," about a " monument," he took so much pains to emphasize. Instead, all her thoughts, not only in her direct response to her brother's message but throughout her encounter with his envoy, appear to be dominated by the enmity motif. And she even makes it clear that victory over his enemies, their destruction, banishment, and submission, is the all-decisive task of his career, the condition on which everything else depends: his undisputed rule over the Height of Ṣapon, the establishment of his sovereignty, the ignition of his " horn." Nor is it admissible to ascribe this attitude to the warlike and impetuous character of Anat or, possibly, to a particular predilection of the narrator of 5AB. A less poignant perhaps, but no less clear, stress of the enmity motif is a characteristic common to Baal and his allies throughout the Ugaritic mythological poems. We recall the utterance of Baal in an encounter with Anat, which we cited above from *4AB*. Equally characteristic is an utterance of Hayin, an outsider in the Ugaritic pantheon, addressed to Baal, related in still another poem (*3AB A* :8-10):

1. ht ibk tmxṣ
2. ht tṣmt ṣrtk
3. tqḥ mlk ʿlmk
4. drkt dt drdrk

1. When thine enemy thou shalt cut up,
2. When thou shalt crush thy rival,
3. Thou wilt obtain thy kingdom eternal,
4. Thy reign forever and ever.[81]

It seems indeed that we have here particularly lucid testimony to the complete integration of the several motifs we have been able to discern as underlying the building saga. For in the mouth of Hayin, the master-builder, the above utterance cannot but imply that Baal's final victory over his enemies and his obtaining "eternal" kingdom are necessary prerequisites for the fulfillment of his desire which the master-builder was called upon to help bring about—his desire for a house on the Height of Ṣapon cast of precious metals.[81a]

[81] Even if the two couplets were intended as independent clauses, they would imply a causal nexus. I believe, however, that we should posit *ht* as a particle introducing a temporal or conditional clause, thus being related to *hm* (*UG*, 11.1); it is tempting to combine *ht* with Hebrew and Aramaic *hen*, "when, if," and to analyze it as *hitta* < *hinta*.

[81a] The present writer had arrived at this understanding of *3AB A* before he was made to realize by the evidence of the *C* fragment that, in destroying Prince Sea, Baal eliminates, with the crucial help of Hayin, not just an "enemy," but an actual "rival" of his building plan; cf. above, pp. 15 ff.

IV. *EL CONSENTS TO ANAT'S DEMAND*—PARALLELS

An especially vexing break in the text of *5AB*, we have seen, deprives us of a decisive kind of evidence concerning the relationship of this text to that of *2AB*. Specifically, it deprives us of the answer which El gave to Anat when, following her threats, she put before him the " complaint " that Baal had no house. For if the narrator made El answer in benevolent terms, he could not possibly have told, subsequently, how Baal, who would thus have already obtained El's approval of his plan through his sister Anat, undertook to obtain the same approval through his mother Athirat. In other words, if El answered Anat's request in the affirmative, this would prove conclusively that the narrator of *5AB* could not very well have been the same as the narrator of *2AB*; and that, accordingly, the two texts must be seen to represent different narratives of the building epic with Baal as the leading hero of the plot, rather than consecutive portions of the same narrative. By the same token, if the two texts were narrated by the same poet, as parts of a single consecutive narrative, he would necessarily have related in *5AB* how El rejected Anat's intercession in behalf of Baal and thus made it necessary for his son to arrange for a new intercession, this time by his mother.

Deprived of the direct testimony that would have been furnished had El's reply been preserved on the tablet, we are obliged to guide ourselves by a working hypothesis based on such circumstantial evidence as is available. Such a hypothesis appears to favor the assumption that El did answer in the affirmative and that, hence, we actually have here to do with two different, though closely related, narratives of how Baal succeeded in building for himself an extraordinary kind of house. We have already referred to some of the circumstances in support of this assumption; we may now refer to yet another circumstance, perhaps the most conclusive one. It is that the two essential turns in the scene between El and Anat as described in *5AB*, namely, Anat's threat to her father and her plea on behalf of her brother, have verbal parallels of the closest kind in two similar scenes, in both of which the outcome is undeniably of positive, affirmative character.

A Parallel from Daniel. One of the parallel scenes is contained in the Ugaritic Daniel poem. Since the poems themselves, that of *5AB* and that of Daniel, are entirely heterogeneous in subject matter, the parallelism in question should not be confused with the phenomenon of topical reiteration often found within the same poem or with that of topical interdependence exhibited by related poems, such as *5AB* and *2AB*, or *5AB* and *6AB*. Rather, we are here faced with a particularly instructive instance of the stylistic device, widely employed by Ugaritic narrators as we have seen, whereby a given literary formula may be found to describe a given psychological or dramatic situation even when occurring in completely diverse general settings.

In the case of the parallelism before us, the psychological-dramatic similarity of the two scenes is further enhanced by the identity of the chief actors involved. In both instances, Anat seeks to obtain El's approval for an objective she desires: promotion of Baal's plan in *5AB*, acquisition of Aqhat's bow in Daniel. In both instances, too, Anat is determined to sweep aside any reluctance or disapproval on the part of El by threatening him with physical violence. And in both poems, accordingly, she is made to intimidate her father by an identical harangue of eight stichoi (*5AB* E : 27-33 = *3D* 6 : 7-12). As it happens, the corresponding passage is damaged in both tablets; even so there can be no question but that Anat's statement is the same in both scenes, while some of the stichoi may be, and others have been, restored beyond reasonable doubt:

1. al tśmx al tśmx . . .
2. am[xṣ ẓr] qdqdk
3. ašhlk śbt[k dm]
4. śbt dqnk mmʿ-m

1. " Rejoice not, rejoice not! . . .
2. I shall wou[nd the crown] of thy scalp.[82]
3. I shall make [thy] gray hair flow [with blood]
4. Thy gray beard with gore! "[83]

Again, in both scenes El is made to reply to this threat in identical words (*5AB* E : 35-36 = *3D* 6 : 16-17), and in words so timid and appeasing as to make it clear that he is about to yield to his daughter's demand:

1. ydʿtk bt k anšt
2. k in b ilht qlṣt

[82] Cf., as to the application of *ẓr*, Arabic idioms like *ẓahr al-lisān*, " the upper surface of the tongue " (similarly, *ẓahr al-qadam*, *ẓahr al-kaff*), and, as to the phrase as a whole, as well as to its connection with the following stichos, Psalms 68 (which has long since been seen to re-echo imagery characteristic of Ugaritic mythology): 22, " God will smite (*yimḥaṣ*) the head of his enemies, the hairy scalp (*qoḏqōḏ*)," etc.; cf. also Jeremiah 48 : 45*c*. In Ugaritic itself, cf. *hlm qdqd*, also *ylm qdqd* (*3AB* 21, 24); is perhaps *2AB* 7 : 4 to be restored *y*[*mxṣ*] *l ẓr qdqdh?*

[83] See " Negation," 240 f. and n. 17.

1. "I know thee, my daughter, that thou art amiable,
2. (And) that there is no maligner among goddesses." [84]

Here the parallelism comes to an end, but only because the narrators have followed a different arrangement of their materials. For, in *5AB*, Anat has not yet told her father what she wants him to do for her; accordingly, the narrator makes El here add another stichos:

mh taršn l btlt ʿnt

"What is it thou desirest, oh Virgin Anat?" [85]

—whereupon Anat proceeds to put before him her plea in behalf of Baal, which plea forms the second of our parallels, as we shall see. In the Daniel poem, on the other hand, the narrator makes Anat, first, convey to

[84] On *anšt* (here no doubt a perfect: *'aništi*), see "Negation," n. 30. Virolleaud renders *bt* "ô ma fille"; more likely, however, "my daughter" should be understood as forming an apposition to the preceding suffix (*k*); cf. *ġry il ṣpn* discussed above (p. 51); also *tbkyk ab* (above, n. 7); *ir*]*tk nʿmn* (above; n. 43), and *tḫmk il* (below, n. 91). On the whole, the first couplet was properly rendered by Aistleitner, *op. cit.*, "Ich weiss von dir, Tochter, dass du hold bist." An instructive parallel may be found in an utterance of Keret to his son Ilḥau: *axtk ydʿt k rḥmt*, "Thy sister, I know that she is compassionate" (*2K* 1-2 : 32; cf. *LK*, p. 26); it is possible, however, that, in phrases of this kind, *ydʿ* was used in an endearing or flattering sense, in which case *k* would have to be rendered "for, because"—"I esteem thee, my daughter, for thou art amiable" and "Thy sister I esteem, for she is compassionate." In lieu of *qlṣt*, *D* has *qlṣ*; in the interpretation suggested here, the masculine might be no less correct than the feminine. I believe that the word should be combined with the (dissimilated?) root *qls* employed in Hebrew in the sense of "to mock, to malign, to deride" (see Ges.-Buhl, *s. v.*); some such sense may well be intended in *2AB* 3 : 12 (*yqlṣn*) and 6 : 13 (*qlṣn*); cf. Arabic *qalaṣa*, dialectically *qalasa*, "to become agitated (by a tendency to vomit)," also "to spring, leap, bound."

[85] In *1AB* 2 : 14, the identical question is uttered by Mot when he is pressed by Anat concerning the whereabouts of Baal; it would seem that there, too, the question is intended to pacify the angry goddess.

El her demand concerning Aqhat and his bow and, second, reinforce her demand by the threatening harangue which we have cited.[86] Hence, he makes El yield as soon as the threats are uttered. Together with the appeasing stichos already referred to, El's full reply to Anat reads as follows (*3D* 6 : 16-20):

1. yd'tk bt k anšt
2. k in b ilht qlṣ[t]
3. w tb' bt xnp lb
4. [ti]xd d iṯ b kbdk
5. tšt [d iṯ b] irtk
6. dṯ ydṯ m'qbk
7. [qm] btlt 'nt

1. "I know thee, my daughter, that thou art amiable,
2. [And] that there is no maligner among goddesses;
3. While a daughter's demand flatters the heart.[87]
4. Thou [mayest] (then) take whatever is in thy mind,

---

[86] See *2D* 6 : 51 (*tlšn aqht ġzr*) and cf. Ginsberg *BASOR, 98*, 23.

[87] This rendering of the difficult stichos is offered, as a conjecture, for want of anything better; cf. Virolleaud: "'Et cours (vers) la maison du *ḫnp lb*'; ou bien 'et cours (ô ma) fille,'" etc. Should the conjecture prove substantiated, we would have here a sort of epigrammatic truism, if not indeed a popular proverb (cf. 1 Samuel 10 : 12; 24 : 14), skillfully applied by El as a means of appeasing the threatening Anat. In itself, it is not inconceivable that *tb'*, if its primary meaning was "to pursue, to follow, to go after" (Arabic *taba'a*), should have developed semantically, on the one hand, in the sense of "to depart" and even, it seems, "to die" (*1K* 1 : 14), and, on the other, in that of "to ask, to demand" (Aramaic *tĕḇa'*, Mishnaic *tāḇa'*); WS *rdp* covers a similar range of meaning; cf. especially "to pursue (a desire), to seek after, to long after." Nor is it inconceivable that *xnp* would correspond with NWS *ḥnp* (Arabic *ḥanīf* has universally been recognized as a loan word) in the sense of "to flatter, to cajole"; cf. Levy, *s. vv. ḥānēp̄, ḥănūp̄â*; indeed, the biblical phrase *ḥanp̄ê lēḇ* (Job 36 : 13) may best be understood as "cajolers, flatterers, hypocrites" (contrasted to those who "hearken," *v.* 11, as well as to those who "hearken not," *v.* 12).

5. Accomplish [whatever is in] thy heart.[88]
6. Thy heel shall surely crush
7. [Any adversary] of the Virgin Anat." [89]

Thus the threat has proved effective in the extreme. For Anat has now obtained El's approval of any action she might take in order to compel Aqhat to surrender his bow in her favor. In effect, El not only has given her *carte blanche* to proceed as she pleases, he has even wished her good luck. Small wonder that, upon returning to Aqhat after her visit with El, the goddess appears to be in the best of humor or, as the narrator puts it (*3D* 6 : 22), " the Virgin Anat laughs."

A Parallel from 2AB. The second parallel involving Anat's plea is contained in a corresponding scene between El and Athirat as described in *2AB*. Here, how-

[88] For the locution, cf. the biblical counterpart in 1 Samuel 14 : 7, " do all that is in thy heart " ; similarly 2 Samuel 7 : 3; and Psalms 20 : 5, " may He grant thee according to thine own heart." Virolleaud, mistaking the nature of *diṯ* in *l.* 4, and restoring *l.* 5 to read *tśt b*[*m(?)*] *ertk*, renders the couplet " Prends le *deš* dans ton foie; tu le mettras dans (?) ta poitrine " (*Danel*, p. 226).

[89] Better perhaps: " May thy heel crush (or tread) [him who opposes] the Virgin Anat." It is obvious that *dṯ* must be combined with Hebrew *d-š*, " to crush, to beat small, to tread, to trample " (*Isaiah* 41 : 15, " thou shalt *crush* mountains and beat them small " ; Habakkuk 3 : 12, " thou treadst the earth in wrath, in anger thou *tramplest* the nations " ; Job 39 : 15, " the wild beast may *crush* them ") and Arabic *dāṯa*: *dayyaṯa*, " to make smooth, even (a road), to render submissive, gentle (a man) "; hence *mudayyaṯ*, " (a road) beaten, trodden, made even." (We are thus led to infer that two different roots, related and partly synonymous in meaning, had coalesced in Hebrew *d-š*; namely, Sem. *d-ṯ*, in the sense just stated, and Sem. *d-š*, Arabic *dāsa*, " to thresh (grain), to beat out, to tread, to trample "; for another instance of this kind, cf. Ges.-Buhl, *s. v. šāmar*.) In *m'qb* we would seem to have the Ugaritic equivalent of Arabic *'aqib*, Hebrew *'āqēḇ*; possibly a nomen instrumenti in the sense of " boot, sandal " ; cf. *na'l mu'aqqabah* in Arabic. For the restoration *qm*, see above, p. 43 (9) and n. 53; in the present context, however, a singular would seem more natural than a plural.

ever, the agreement in verbal expression is effected not merely by a literary formula being employed to depict a given situation—such as exacting consent by threats of physical violence—within otherwise diverse settings, but rather by the similarity, indeed the sameness, of the settings themselves. For, in *5AB* and *2AB*, the same petition is placed before the same god in behalf of the same petitioner. That is to say, in both poems El is asked to grant Baal the right to build a house for himself. Here, therefore, the identity in the wording of the plea must be accounted for by the topical affinity and interdependence of the two poems. However, it is remarkable that the verbal agreement should extend beyond the plea of the petitioner, Baal, to that of the bearers of the petition, that is, to the personal intercessions of Anat and Athirat, respectively. Having uttered a series of dire threats to her father, the ferocious Anat replies to his timid question " What is it thou desirest, oh Virgin Anat? " in the same words as those which, in *2AB*, the gentle Athirat addresses to her spouse, who, surprised by her sudden visit at his residence, had just offered her a most affectionate welcome. Taking as a basis the text of *5AB* (E : 38 ff.), and listing in parentheses the variants offered in *2AB* (4-5 : 41 ff.), we find the passage under discussion to read as follows:

1. tḥmk il ḥkm ḥkmk (ḥkmt)
2. ʿm ʿlm ḥyt ḥẓt

3. tḥmk mlkn aliyn bʿl
4. ṯpṭn (w) in d ʿlnh

5. klnyy (klnyn) qśh nbln
6. klnyy (klnyn) nbl ksh.

It seems obvious that we have come here upon two instances of the root *tḥm* employed as a verb.[90] We notice that, in the first of the two instances (*l.* 1), the following noun qualifies, appositionally, the pronominal suffix which here reflects the direct object, *taḥamaka 'ila* (acc.), " (Thus) spoke (to) thee, El "; while in the second instance (*l.* 3) the following substantive introduces the agent of the verb: *taḥamaka malkunā* (nom.), " (Thus) spoke (to) thee our King." [91] We further notice that each of the two readings, *ḥkmk* and *ḥkmt*, although suggesting a difference in meaning and construction, makes good sense in the present context: *ḥakama ḥukmuka*, " may thy judgment be wise," and *ḥukma(?) ḥakamta*, " mayest thou act wisely " or perhaps, " thou are surely wise." If the plus of *w* be original, the following phrase would qualify Baal rather than " our Judge." We cannot be sure what *klny* means. It is tempting to see in it a noun with a double afformative, *n* (*ān*) and *y* (*āy* or *īy*), derived from the verb *kll*, " to be perfect, complete," or perhaps from *k-l*, " to contain, to provide," or else from *ykl*, " to be able, potent," and to surmise that it is a title or epithet of Baal, comparable with " King " and " Judge." [92] Our rendering

[90] So also Ginsberg, in *2AB* (*The Ugaritic Texts*, p. 30; also p. 48), but elsewhere " message of " (*1K* 125, etc.); Aistleitner, on the contrary, renders *tḥmk* here as " dein Entschluss," but elsewhere in *5AB* " es entbietet . . . es lässt sagen." See above, n. 41.

[91] Possibly (but not probably; see n. 84): " Thus spoke to thee, oh El—mayest thou," etc.; on *malkuna* (*malikna*?) and, below in the text, *ḥukmuka* (*ḥukumka?*), see above, n. 69.

[92] Cf. the fusion of the afformatives *ôn* and *îy* in Hebrew (Bauer-Leander, p. 501), *ān* and *īy* in Arabic (Wright, *1*, 164 f.), *ān* and *āy* in Syriac (Nöldeke, *Syr. Gr.*, p. 75), and *ān* and *ī* in Biblical-Aramaic (Bauer-Leander, p. 197); in Ugaritic both *(ā)n and (ā/ī)y* are employed as afformatives (*UG*, 7. 26 f.; cf. *JBL*, *55*, 24, n. 4), while *ilny-m*, paralleled with *il-m* (*5AB* D:78; cf. above, n. 78) may well represent another

"Sovereign" is entirely conjectural, of course. At any rate, the suffix *n* fits better with the same suffix in the two preceding epithets, as well as with the first person plural of the following *nbl*, than does *y*. The whole passage may therefore be rendered thus:

1. (Thus) spoke (to) thee, El—mayest thou act wisely,
2. Mayest thou forever live and prosper!—
3. (Thus) spoke (to) thee our King, Aliyan Baal;
4. Our Judge, over whom there is none;
5. Our Sovereign, whose goblet we would fain bear,
6. Our Sovereign—we would fain bear his cup.[93]

What it was that Baal "spoke" to El is quoted verbatim in what immediately follows in both tablets: the petition or "complaint" which Baal has instructed his sister and his mother, respectively, to put before his father. Although such a verbatim quotation is, as a rule, introduced by an authentication formula of two

instance of the same fusion (*'ilānā/īy*); perhaps also *ulny* || *'ẓmny* [*sic!*], in *3AB, A* :5, and *b'lny* || *krt, 3K* 5 :20 (considered by Ginsberg, *LK*, p. 43, as a suffix first person dual; cf. *UG*, 5. 2; it would be curious indeed that three or four words of undoubtedly related meaning should be found to end in *ny*, and that only in one of them, *b'lny*, but certainly not in the others, *ilny, ulny, 'ẓmny*, and *klny*, this ending should represent a pronominal suffix; cf. also Virolleaud, *Syria, 21* (1940), 251 f.); I have long felt that *aliyn* merely represents *aliy* + *ān* (see the reference above, n. 40). Perhaps we have here to do with a formative of intensity or superlativeness, as in Aramaic *'illāyā*, Hebrew *'elyôn* < *'elyān*, "Most High." Since, in accordance with its variant (*klnyn*), the final *y* of *klnyy* must be seen to represent a possessive suffix of the first person singular—that is *k-lānāyī* or *k-lānīyī*—we would have here another instance of *y* serving as a mater lectionis in final position (see above, n. 42).

[93] In *nbln* – *nbl* we would seem to have yet another instance of a pair of optatives, of which the first is strengthened by the particle *na* (cf. above, n. 59). I take it that, in parallel with *ks*, "cup," *qš* (*qaśā?*) represents the masculine counterpart of Hebrew *qaśwâ*, "goblet, tumbler," or the like. The bearing of Baal's cup is apparently a symbol of submission to his authority and also, no doubt, of the high position of the bearer; cf. Genesis 40 :21; Nehemiah 2 :1.

stichoi constituting part of the quotation, as we have seen, it is obvious that the instance before us represents an exception to the rule, both as to the length and the connotation of the formula. The whole tenor of the passage just cited, especially the verbs and pronouns in the first person, makes it clear beyond a doubt that here the bearer of the petition is made to preface its presentation in her own words. By referring to the petitioner in the exalting epithets " our King," " our Judge," " our Sovereign," Athirat, in *2AB*, and Anat, in *5AB*, are here made to emphasize their strong personal endorsement of Baal's request which they are about to put before El. Incidentally, we learn here once again how all-inclusive Athirat's and Anat's alliance with Baal was held to be in Ugaritic mythology: far beyond their promotion of his building plan, they eulogize him as if he, rather than El, were the supreme god of the pantheon.

Because of the break in the tablet of *5AB*, we may never know exactly how the narrator made El react to Baal's petition as put before him by Anat and to her personal endorsement of that petition. But we do know how El reacted to the same petition put before him by Athirat and to the identical personal endorsement. Apparently without a trace of enthusiasm, and perhaps even with a grain of grudge, El did yield to Athirat's plea in behalf of her son. In effect, we recall, he told her that he would not object if a handmaiden of hers would ready bricks with which to build " a house for Baal."

It is proposed here that each of the two parallels which we have considered would suffice to demonstrate that, in *5AB*, El's reply to Anat was as positive and affirmative as it is in Daniel on the one hand, and in *2AB* on the other. (*a*) Had the narrator of *5AB* related how El disregarded Anat's intimidation, it is all but inconceivable that he would have put into her mouth exactly the same series of threats, and would have made El respond in the very same timid words, which, in Daniel, lead up to a complete yielding by her father to the goddess' demand. (*b*) Again, had the narrator of *5AB* described how El turned a deaf ear to his daughter's intercession in behalf of his son, it is equally inconceivable that he would have made her preface Baal's petition by precisely the same endorsement by which, in *2AB*, El was persuaded to give his consent. Combined, the two parallels render the inference of El's yielding to Anat's threats and, by the same token, his submission to her intercession all but unavoidable.

V. SUMMARY AND OUTLOOK

In the foregoing study an attempt has been made, not to offer a complete analysis of *5AB*, but merely to prepare the groundwork for such an analysis. In doing so, we have been led to recognize certain basic trends and to solidify one or two general directives that may prove helpful for a critical interpretation of other mythological texts as well. In retrospect, it may be permissible to recapitulate the main results, even though final claim for their validity could be made only by demonstrating the extent to which they are borne out by all the pertinent text material available.

1. The primary motif underlying the several poems bearing on the building epic, as well as related poems, is an alliance of certain gods with Baal and a corollary alliance of these gods against his enemies. While thus holding the most prominent position and occupying the center of the stage in the narratives concerned, Baal is nevertheless subordinated to El, at least in a perfunctory sense—as if the ethnic or ideological conditions which led to the formation of the religious-epical motif were still in flux. In other words, the Ugaritic poems under discussion seem to reflect an acute crisis, in consequence of which the supreme authority over the pantheon hitherto held by El tends to shift from this aging god to his son Baal. Hence the great prevalence of intrigue and connivance in the dramatic development of the several narratives.

2. Another motif, clearly less primary but certainly no less effective than the alliance-enmity motif, is that

of the control of precious metals and also, it would seem, of the art of producing metalwork. Here, again, the poems appear to reflect a recent crisis in the Ugaritic community, but a crisis of socio-economic, rather than ethnic or cosmological, nature. We may say that it is a crisis occasioned by the advance of technology, the emergence of the smith and the foundry.

3. Specifically, the theme of the building epic might thus be understood as having grown out of an endeavor to explain, etiologically, how the simplicity of old had come to be replaced, in Ugaritic temples and no doubt in the Ugaritic community in general, by the new fashion of elaborate and luxurious designs, by the wondrous fixtures and furnishings and vessels produced by the new process of metallurgical smelting and molding.

4. If Baal was now to obtain absolute sovereignty, if, after overwhelming his enemies and subduing his rivals, he was to win supremacy over all the gods, it was only fitting that he should have been the god who had inaugurated the new age of metallurgy by inviting the Egyptian artisan-god Hayin to build for him a house of gold and silver and lapis lazuli. He still was in need of El's consent, but this was now a mere formality to be obtained, if necessary, by duress and trickery. By the same token, if El was to continue wielding unquestioned authority and to retain his supreme place in the pantheon, it was just as fitting that it should have been he, and not Baal, who introduced the new age and who ordered Hayin to build him a house "of stone of splendor."

5. In *5AB*, column 3, we come upon the beginning of a narrative of the building epic with Baal as its hero. It starts with a message from Baal to Anat, in which the

god invites his sister to ally herself with his cause; it ends with, or rather breaks up in, the middle of a scene describing how Baal dispatched his envoy to Hayin, so that we do not know how the narrative ended. Another narrative of the same epic, also with Baal as its hero, is contained in *2AB*. Here, on the contrary, we have the end of the narrative but not the beginning—the first lines preserved on the tablet belonging to a scene in which Baal sends a request to his mother Athirat to put before El his plea for a house.

6. To a considerable extent, therefore, the two narratives cover the same ground, often in identical descriptions and discourses. Told by different narrators, no doubt in different Ugaritic locales and perhaps also in different ages, it is quite natural that we should find an equally considerable amount of deviation in the structure as well as in the substance of the dramatic action, an outstanding example of their disagreement being that in *5AB* it is Anat who puts Baal's plea before El and obtains his consent to the plan, while in *2AB* it is Athirat.

7. Still another narrative of the Ugaritic building epic—presumably originating in a circle of priests of El, unlike the two preceding narratives, which may be assumed to represent the tradition of priests of Baal—seems to be preserved in *6AB*. Here, at any rate, the hero is El rather than Baal. Yet this narrative, too, appears to have covered to a considerable extent the same ground, often using the same discourses, as that of *5AB*. For, just as Baal in the two other narratives, so in *6AB* El invites Anat to ally herself with him and appoints the Egyptian Hayin to be the architect of a new kind of house. The points of topical interdependence would

no doubt have been even more pronounced had the three tablets, and especially that of *6AB*, been less fragmentary.

8. Finally, to judge from the two fragments of *3AB* now available, the narrator of this poem seems to have followed a pattern, or a tradition, even more clear-cut than that of any of the other poems. For he appears to have told, more bluntly and explicitly than his fellow narrators, of an acute antagonism between El and Baal, and to have interwoven this motif with that of metallurgy by making the Hephaistos play a decisive part in both. In employing a weapon fashioned for him by Hayin, Baal eliminates a rival sponsored by the supreme god, a pretender (to the new kind of house) sanctioned by the authority of El.[94]

9. That several different narratives of the Ugaritic building epic should have been found at the same site—the library of the earthly temple of Baal exhumed by the excavators of Ras Shamra—and very possibly copied, if not first committed to writing, by the same hand, is not without analogy in the various archives and libraries exhumed in, or transmitted from, the ancient Near East.[95] Perhaps the most remarkable analogy is exhi-

[94] Specifically, by the evidence from the *A* fragment (see above, n. 23, and the Repertory, No. 18), the narrator of *3AB* would appear to have incorporated in his version of the building saga an etiological myth reflecting the expulsion of an enemy who had invaded Ugarit from the sea region and whose god was named, or nicknamed, "Prince Sea" and "Chieftain River."

[95] Among the "Fragments mythologiques" (see above, n. 22), Virolleaud has published two small pieces, marked *RS 5180*, which he holds to have been broken off from a single tablet. One of these pieces (*A*) may easily be recognized as part of a message closely parallel with, and at the same time quite diverse from, Baal's message to Anat which we have considered in detail, that is, *5AB* 3:1-28; the other piece (*B*) appears to re-echo the scene of Anat's massacre as described in *5AB*, column 2.

bited by the collection of Hebrew writings preserved in the Old Testament, into which four different documents have found their way, all pertaining to a " house " or " dwelling place " of God: a narrative of the building of the Tabernacle in the wilderness under Moses (Exodus 25 ff.); a story of the building of the Jerusalem Temple under Solomon (1 Kings 6 ff.); a different version of the same story told by the Chronicler (2 Chronicles 2 ff.); and a vision about the Jerusalem Temple of the future under a " Prince " (Ezekiel 40 ff.). To make the analogy particularly suggestive, in three of the Hebrew documents, those pertaining to the past, the art of the smith and the foundry producing a vast variety of works in gold, silver and copper forms the outstanding architectural feature of the " house of the Lord "—a correspondence that would deserve scholarly scrutiny of the minutest kind.

Virolleaud was therefore led to remark that these two fragments " appartenant visiblement au même cycle que *V AB* . . . et pouvant être considérée comme une autre version ou un autre épisode de la même légende " (*ibid.*, p. 12). In terms of the present inquiry, it would be more precise to say that we simply seem to deal here with remnants of still another narrative of the building saga, i. e., in addition to the four narratives which we have discerned (*5AB*, *2AB*, *6AB*, *3AB*).

VI. REPERTORY OF THE TREATED TEXT UNITS

1. *A Scene of Baal's Wedding*

5AB A: 9-25 pp. 7-11

He proceeds to felicitate him and bid him drink;
He puts a cup in his hand,
A jar in both his hands,
With a rope strong (and) supple
Which he stretches out heavenward.
(It's) a cup of betrothal no woman has ever seen,
A jar no goddess has ever beheld:
A thousand pitchers it contains of wine,
A myriad are blended in its mixture.
(Now) he rises to chant, and to sing,
With cymbals, a pleasant song;
He sings aloud, good in voice:
" Baal has come up to the Fastness of Ṣapon,
Baal will visit his lasses;
He will behold Pidriya, daughter of Ar,
Even Ṭilliya, daughter of Rabb . . ."

2. *Baal's Invitation to Anat*

5AB C: 1-28 pp. 21-55; p. 65 f.

Ye [shall] put a gem on her breast:
As a token of the love of Aliyan Baal,
Of the loyal[ty] (?) of Pidriya, daughter of Ar,
Of the devotion of Ṭilliya, daughter of Rabb,
Of the love of Arṣiya, daughter of Ya'buddar.
Like stewards then do ye enter:
At the feet of Anat crouch ye and fall down,

Prostrate yourselves and honor her.
And proclaim ye to the Virgin Anat,
Declare to the Yamamat of the People:

"(Thus) spoke Aliyan Baal,
(Thus) said Aliy Qardam:
'Strike thou the warriors to the ground,
Put to the dust the repellers,
Pour out submission to the core of the earth,
Overwhelm insurrection to the core of the land.

Let thy compassion (for me) constrain thee:
Let it unite thee with me.
Thy feet shall gallop toward me,
Thy tread shall stamp out impudence.

I have (at heart) a thing I wish to tell thee,
A matter I wish to convey to thee.
(It's) a thing about wood,
And a secret about stone.
(It's) the contention of heaven with the earth,
Of the deep with the stars.
(It's) stone of splendor, which the heavens have not known,
A thing that men have not known,
And the multitudes of the earth have not perceived.
(It concerns) a monument that I do desire,
Amid the mountain of mine, God of Ṣapon,
In Holiness, on the mount of my inheritance,
In Delight, on the hill of Endeavor.'"

3. *Anat's Anxiety for Baal*

5AB D:34-35; 43-44 pp. 57-59

What enemies have risen unto Baal?
What rivals, unto the Rider of Clouds? . . .
(Thus) I will batter on and inherit gold!

4. *Athirat's Anxiety and Recovery*

2AB 2:21-28 **n. 73**

(Then) she lifted her voice and exclaimed:
" Why did Aliyan Baal come?
Why did the Virgin Anat come?
Does a smiter s[mi]te my children?
[Does] a ba[tterer batter the f]lock of my kin? "
(Yet) when Athirat beheld the [shadow] of silver,
The shadow of silver and the gl[itter] of gold,
Then did Lady Athirat of the Sea rejoice.

5. *Anat Offers Advice to Baal through His Envoy*

5AB D:45-48 pp. 58-62

Let Baal banish from the Height of Ṣapon
(Anyone) who makes trouble and withholds his obedience;
Let him expel him from the seat of his kingdom.
Yea, let him pluck out from the throne of his reign
Whatever enemies have risen unto Baal,
(Whatever) rivals, unto the Rider of Clouds.

6. *Baal's Envoy Confirms Anat's Fears*

5AB D:49-50 p. 64 f.

Forsooth, enemies have risen unto Baal,
Rivals, unto the Rider of Clouds!

7. *Anat Accepts Baal's Bidding*

5AB D:65-75 pp. 67-70

And there answered the Virgin Anat,
There replied the [Yamamat] of the People:
" [When] I strike the warriors to the ground,

Put to the dust the repellers,
Pour out submission to the core of the earth,
Overcome resistance to the core of the land,
Then will [Aliyan] Baal establish his sovereignty,
Then will [the Rider of Cloud]s ignite his [h]orn!
I [indeed] will strike the warriors to the ground,
I will put to the dust the repellers,
Will pour out submission to the core of the earth,
Overcome resistance to the core of the land!

8. *Anat Threatens Her Father*

5AB E:27-33 = *3 D* 6:7-12 p. 74

" Rejoice not, rejoice not! . . .
I shall wou[nd the crown] of thy scalp!
I shall make [thy] gray hair flow [with blood],
Thy gray beard with gore! "

9. *El Appeases His Daughter*

5AB E:35-37 pp. 74 f.

I know thee, my daughter, that thou art amiable,
(And) that there is no maligner among goddesses.
What is it thou desirest, oh Virgin Anat?

10. *Anat (Athirat) Intercedes for Baal*

5AB E:38-42 = *2AB* 4-5:41-46 pp. 78-80

(Thus) spoke (to) thee, El—mayest thou act wisely,
Mayest thou forever live and prosper!—
(Thus) spoke (to) thee our King, Aliyan Baal;
Our Judge, over whom there is none;
Our Sovereign, whose goblet we would fain bear,
Our Sovereign—we would fain bear his cup.

11. *Anat (Athirat) Puts Baal's Plea before El*

5AB E : 46-51 = *2AB* 4-5 : 50-57 pp. 30 f.; 5

Woe, there is no house unto Baal like (unto) the gods,
(Nor) a court like (unto) the sons of Athirat:
(Like) the dwelling of El that shelters his sons,
(Like) the dwelling of Lady Athirat of the Sea!
(No) dwelling for (his) perfect brides:
A dwelling for Pidriya, daughter of Ar,
A shelter for Ṭilliya, daughter of Rabb,
A dwelling for Arṣiya, daughter of Ya'buddar!

12. *El Gives His Consent*

2AB 4-5 : 61-62 p. 4

Lo, let a handmaiden of Athirat ready bricks,
(Thus) a house may be built for Baal like the gods.

13. *Mot Apprised by Baal*

2AB 8 : 40-42 p. 2

My house I have built [of silver,
Of gold I have wrought my pa]lace!

14. *El Commissions Hayin*

6AB 3 : 27-29 n. 21

Pray [raise a palace],
In the midst [of the Fastness of Ṣapon,
And] build [a house of silver and gold].

15. *An Encounter between Baal and Anat*

4AB 2 : 13-25 n. 49; pp. 43-45

When he lifts his eyes and looks,
When he beholds the Virgin Anat,
The [gra]ceful sweetness of his sister,

Baal runs to meet her, then he halts;
(Now) he kneels at her feet and falls down.
Then he raises his voice and exclaims:
" May my sister live!
And may the horn of the Virgin Anat sway!
Thy scourging horn Baal will anoint,
Baal will anoint it with hardness:
We shall thrust to the ground my enemies,
And to the dust the adversaries of thy brother."

16. *Athtar's Dirge over El's Decision*

3AB C:19-21 n. 25b

He has [sn]atched me off, has the Bull El, my father.
I—there be no house [unto me like] (unto) the gods,
[Nor] a court [like (unto) the hol]y ones.
After a domicile I am to seek of my own accord,
While the Masterful [and Discerning] one is to toil
At a hou[se for Prince] Sea,
At a palace for Chieftain River.

17. *Hayin Encourages Baal*

3AB A:8-10 p. 71

When thine enemy thou shalt cut up,
When thou shalt crush thy rival,
Thou wilt obtain thy kingdom eternal,
Thy reign forever and ever.

18. *Baal Destroys a Rival with a Weapon Made by Hayin*

3AB A:11-28 n. 23 *

A The Skillful one—a staff he fashions,

* See now the writer's article "How Baal Destroyed a Rival," *JAOS*, 1947, pp. 195 ff.

And pronounces its design:
" Thy name, yea thine, is 'He-Will-Expel! He-Will-Expel!'
Let him expel Sea!
Let him expel Sea from his throne,
River, from the seat of his reign!
Thou shalt swoop in the hand of Baal,
Like a vulture in his fingers!
Let him strike Prince Sea on the shoulder,
Between the arms, Chieftain River! "

Swoops the staff in the hand of Baal,
Like a vulture in his fingers.
He strikes Prince Sea on the shoulder,
Between the arms, Chieftain River.

Sea has withstood,
He does not bend,
His hips do not quiver,
His figure does not waver.

B The Skillful one—a staff he fashions,
And pronounces its design:
" Thy name, yea thine, is 'Ah, He-Will-Force-Out! Ah, He-Will-Force-Out!'
Let him force out Sea!
Let him force out Sea from his throne,
River, from the seat of his reign!
Thou shalt swoop in the hand of Baal,
Like a vulture in his fingers!
Let him strike Prince Sea on the head,
Between the eyes, Chieftain River!
Then will Sea sink down
And will fall to the ground."

So swoops the staff in the hand of Baal,
Like a vulture in his fingers.

He strikes Prince Sea on the head,
Between the eyes, Chieftain River.

Sea sinks down,
He falls to the ground,
His hips do quiver,
And his figure does waver.

C (Now) Baal routs and deranges Sea,
He destroys Chieftain River into ruin.

19. *Anat's Threat to Aqhat*

2D 6:43-45 n. 43

I shall surely strike thee in (thy) rebellious path;
[Lo,] in (thy) proud path I shall humble thee.
There shall come down thy [repose of hea]rt,
Naaman, astutest of men!

20. *El Empowers Anat over Aqhat*

3D 6:16-20 pp. 76 f.

"I know thee, my daughter, that thou art amiable,
(And) that there is no maligner among goddesses;
While a daughter's demand flatters the heart.
Thou [mayest] (then) take whatever is in thy mind,
Accomplish [whatever is in] thy heart.
Thy heel shall surely crush
[Any adversary] of the Virgin Anat."

LIST OF ABBREVIATIONS

1AB, in Charles Virolleaud, "Un poème phénicien de Ras-Shamra," *Syria, 12* (1931), 193 ff.

*1*AB*, in Charles Virolleaud, "La mort de Baal," *Syria, 15* (1934), 305 ff.

2AB, in Charles Virolleaud, "Un nouveau chant du poème d'Alein Baal," *Syria, 13* (1932), 113 ff.

3AB, in Charles Virolleaud, "La révolte de Košer contre Baal," *Syria, 16* (1935), 29 ff.; and "Le dieu 'Aštar," *Syria, 24* (1944-45), 1 ff.

4AB, in Charles Virolleaud, "Anat et la génisse," *Syria, 17* (1936), 150 ff.

5AB, in Charles Virolleaud, *La déesse Anat* (Paris, 1938).

6AB, in Charles Virolleaud, *La déesse Anat*, pp. 91 ff.

BASOR = *Bulletin of the American Schools of Oriental Research.*

Bauer-Leander = ——, *Historische Grammatik der Hebraeischen Sprache* (Halle, 1922).

Bauer-Leander = ——, *Grammatik des Biblisch-Aramaeischen* (Halle, 1927).

BJPES = *Bulletin of the Jewish Palestine Exploration Society.*

Brockelmann = ——, *Grundriss der vergleichenden Gr. d. Sem. Sprachen* (Berlin, 1908-13).

CIS = *Corpus Inscriptionum Semiticarum.*

D (*1D*, *2D*, etc.), in Charles Virolleaud, *La légende phénicienne de Danel* (Paris, 1936).

EI = *The Encyclopaedia of Islam.*

Ges(enius)-Buhl = ——, *Handwoerterbuch ueber das Alte Testament*, 16th ed.

"Incubation" = Obermann, "How Daniel Was Blessed with a Son," *JAOS, 65*, (1946), Supplement No. 6.

JAOS = *Journal of the American Oriental Society.*

JBL = *Journal of Biblical Literature.*

K (*1K*, *2K*, *3K*), in Charles Virolleaud, *La légende de Keret* (Paris, 1936); "Le roi Kéret et son fils," *Syria, 22* (1941), 105 ff., 197 ff.; *23* (1943), 1 ff.; "Le marriage du roi Kéret," *Syria, 23* (1945), 137 ff.

LA = *Lisān al-'Arab* (Cairo, 1882-91).

Lane = ——, *An Arabic-English Lexicon* (Edinburgh, 1863-93).
LK = H. L. Ginsberg, *The Legend of King Keret* (New Haven, 1946).
"Negation" = Obermann, "Sentence Negation in Ugaritic," *JBL, 65,* (1946), 233 ff.
OLZ = *Orientalische Literaturzeitung.*
PL = C. H. Gordon, "The Poetic Literature of Ugarit," *Orientalia, 12* (1943), 31 ff.
RA = *Revue d'assyriologie.*
RÉS = *Revue des Études Semitiques.*
RHR = *Revue de l'Histoire des Religions.*
UG = C. H. Gordon, *Ugaritic Grammar* (Rome, 1940).
Wright = ——, *A Grammar of the Arabic Language,* 3rd ed.
ZAW = *Zeitschrift fuer die alt-test. Wissenschaft.*
ZDMG = *Zeitschrift der Deutschen Morgenlaendischen Gesellschaft.*

INDEX

I. Subjects

Authentication, formula, 24; remains invariable, 36; exception, 80 f.

Baal, central figure of the epic, xvii; his allies, 1; his victory over Mot, 2; his conspiracy against El, 3 f.; his "complaint," 5, 29, 30 f., 80; his marriage, 7 ff.; his choice of Anat as an ally, 12; orders Hayin to proceed with building operations, n. 21; contests a decision of El, 20; his message to Anat, 37 ff.; his commission to her, 53; a gift from him to her, 26 f.; sends his wives to meet her, 42; an encounter between them, 43 ff.; supreme authority shifting to him, 83 (1); his dependency on El a formality, 84 (4). *See also* Building Saga

Baalism, attraction of, xix; mythology of, xx; antagonists of, *ibid.*

Biblical Writings, *see* Hebrew; Old Testament

Brides, Baal's three, 1; mentioned at crucial points of building saga, 11, 20, 30 f.; "perfect brides," 11, 30 (5); gift from, 26 ff.; "lasses," n. 16

Building Saga (Epic), narrative of *5AB* dedicated to, xxi; decisive motif in, 4; *5AB* and *2AB* our chief sources of, 7; their relationship to one another, 12 f., 72 ff., 85 (6); and to *6AB*, 13 f.; n. 21; 85 (7); three episodes of, 12; new material, 14 ff.; peculiarities of, in *3AB*, 17 ff.; Baal hero of, in *2AB* and *5AB*, 84 (5); El hero of, in *6AB*, 14, 85 (7); reflects acute crisis, 83 (1, 2); remmants of a narrative of, n. 95. *See also* Motifs

Canaan, pagan cult of, xviii; gods of, xix

Canannite, Old, as a reference to Ugaritic, xiv; Canaanite Semites of Palestine, xvi, xx

Context, criterion of, xiii f.; usefulness of over-all context, xxi

Cup, in wedding feast, 9 (2); n. 12; "cup of bethrothal," 9 f., 10 (6); n. 10; bearer of, n. 93

Deities, major and minor, 1; connive against Baal's enemies, 3; appearance before a major deity, 32

Daniel (poem), Hayin's role in, 16; a parallel from, 73 ff.

92; signs, 46; n. 26*a*; difficulties of grammatical analysis, xii; dialectic affinity, xiv f.; re-echoes in Hebrew, xv f.; scope of literature, xvii; moves in the sphere of religion, xviii; liking for appositives and asyndeton, 29, 50; cf. n. 32; freedom in word order, 34; position and function of *w*, 34 f., 51; use of *lā* 9, 64, 66; n. 23; use of *-na*, 33; nn. 37, 59, 78, 93; frequency of optative perfects, 47, 59; n. 68; case endings before possessive suffix, n. 69; imperfects as proper names, 31 f.; n. 35; etiquette, diplomatic, n. 28; social, 42; tenet of marital status, 20
Wedding, scene of Baal's, 7 ff.; chant, 9, 10 (13 ff.)
Windows, in Baal's house, 11, 31
Yaʿbuddar, name of, 31 f.; n. 35
Yamamat, "of the People," 35 f.

II. Vocables

III. Passages

1AB

*1*AB*

2AB

3AB

INDEX